Make Us Wave Back

WRITERS ON WRITING
Jay Parini, Series Editor

A good writer is first a good reader. Looking at craft from the inside, with an intimate knowledge of its range and possibilities, writers also make some of our most insightful critics. With this series we will bring together the work of some of our finest writers on the subject they know best, discussing their own work and that of others, as well as concentrating on craft and other aspects of the writer's world.

Poet, novelist, biographer, and critic, Jay Parini is the author of numerous books, including *The Apprentice Lover* and *One Matchless Time: A Life of William Faulkner*. Currently he is D. E. Axinn Professor of English & Creative Writing at Middlebury College.

TITLES IN THE SERIES

Michael Collier
Make Us Wave Back: Essays on Poetry and Influence

Make Us Wave Back

Essays on Poetry and Influence

Michael Collier

The University of Michigan Press

Ann Arbor

2010   2009   2008   2007   4   3   2   1

A CIP catalog record for this book is available from the British Library.

Library of Congress Cataloging-in-Publication Data

Collier, Michael, 1953–
    Make us wave back : essays on poetry and influence / Michael
Collier.
        p.   cm. — (Writers on writing)
    ISBN-13: 978-0-472-09947-4 (cloth : acid-free paper)
    ISBN-10: 0-472-09947-7 (cloth : acid-free paper)
    ISBN-13: 978-0-472-06947-7 (pbk. : acid-free paper)
    ISBN-10: 0-472-06947-0 (pbk. : acid-free paper)
    1. Poetry.   2. Poetics.   I. Title.

PS3553.O474645M35   2007
813'.54—dc22   2007003222

Contents

Preface

IN PUTTING TOGETHER THIS COLLECTION of prose, written over a
period of twenty years, I thought I had no choice but to adopt the
method of the Roman Historian Ninius, who in compiling his
History of Roman Britain "made a heap of all that I found." Surprisingly, in the small heap made from these mostly occasional essays,
I discovered a record of my most important literary influences,
those writers who not only helped me to develop a literary temperament but who also helped to socialize and humanize me. Literary influence differs from the influence of family and place,
which are largely involuntary and often unconscious, and as such
it is the story of a writer's deliberate attempt to find and make
something like a literary home. These essays outline part of my
attempt to make such a place in the world of writing. They also
acknowledge the luck, fortune, and grace that mysteriously preside over the process that has brought me closer to the thing I
most wanted to become, a writer and poet. Not so surprisingly, I
discovered that these essays, especially the shorter ones, are an
expression of certain preoccupations I have had over the years
with the language of poetry and its various traditions, and they
reflect the materials I have used as a teacher of literature and writing. It is my hope that these preoccupations intersect in interesting and perhaps provocative ways with the history of my
influences as it stands so far.

I'm extremely grateful to Jay Parini for offering me the chance to
compile these pieces, and to David Biespiel, who read the manuscript with careful attention, and to my wife, Katherine Branch,
who encouraged me to finish the project and who gave me much
editorial help.

I

One Utterance

DURING THE PERIOD EMERSON WORKED ON "Nature," he thought a great deal about language as a medium for expressing man's relationship to the world. "Words are signs of natural facts," he could say with freshness in those prestructuralist days, and "particular natural facts are symbols of particular spiritual facts." While pondering the nature of language Emerson discovered for himself simple but important evidence that supported his idea that words are signs of natural facts. "Every word," Emerson wrote, "which is used to express a moral or intellectual fact, if traced to its root, is borrowed from some material appearance." Testing Emerson's notion is rewarding. The Latin roots of order are *ordiri* (to lay the warp or to begin) and *ordo* (a line, as in a row of theater seats). The Latin root for complexity, which is the subject of this piece, is found in *plecto* (braiding and plaiting).

Complexity in poetry has its roots in this essential relationship that all language is contained within language, all words within other words. Although poets and prose writers exploit this relationship, poets make it poetry's obsessive subject. Emerson's transcendentalism is only one way of recognizing this relationship. Critic and poet Steve McCaffery in support of "non-intentionality" and "indeterminacy" notes in his essay "Writing as a General Economy," that the "unavoidable presence of words within words contests the notion of writing as a creativity, proposing instead the notion of an indeterminate, extraintentional, differential production." From these similar observations about the braided, interwoven, pattern-making nature of language, McCaffery and Emerson arrive at strikingly different conclusions about the nature of language. Emerson's is a product of hope and optimism, while McCaffery's is a product of doubt and skepticism.

Borges tells us that "universal history is the history of a few metaphors." In suggesting this Borges claims that art is not merely expressive and decorative but that it probes and investigates itself from a few highly selective positions. Risking a simple extrapolation, by way of Emerson, McCaffery, and Borges, I'd like to suggest that all poems contain other poems within them and, furthermore, the universal history of poetry is the history of a few poems. Poetry, in general, is complex, precisely because of these simple notions of containment. When we write, we want to escape, at least partially, from the received meanings of words. "A Rose is a rose is a rose" simplifies the issue by transforming redundancy into pattern and structure, if only to make a point. But the escape is difficult, like swimming fully clothed against the Heraclitean current of time; we are saturated by the medium; it supports us as long as we can keep moving against it but drowns us if we stop.

One of the great poems of the mid–twentieth century that addresses the braided and interwoven relationship that poems have with each other is Philip Larkin's "Sad Steps," with its conscious invocation of Sidney's sonnet 31 from *Astrophil and Stella*. The speaker in Larkin's poem, as he gropes his way "back to bed after a piss," is a paradigm of the common man who finds himself surprised by powerful if not common feelings. He at first seems nothing like Sidney's heartbroken lover who seeks consolation by addressing the moon. Whereas Sidney uses wit and invention and rhetorical guile to align his state of abjection with an otherworldly body, Larkin quickly and directly reveals he is merely "startled by . . . the moon's cleanliness," after which he begins groping for words: "The way the moon dashes through clouds that blow / Loosely as cannon smoke." Then as if a stock simile from Pax Britannica isn't adequate, he gives us direct metaphor: "Lozenge of Love! Medallion of art! / O wolves of memory!" Larkin is drowning albeit ironically in poetic convention and language. It takes him three clichés underscored by three exclamation marks before

4

he comes back to the surface, the original site of his startlement: "No, / One shivers slightly, looking up there." This reclamation of more authentic feeling has the effect of putting him on the same footing as Sidney, who asks calmly, "Oh Moon, tell me, / Is constant love deemed there but want of wit?" Both of these moments mark turns in the rhetorical direction of the poem, and as such Larkin's moment mirrors the volta of Sidney's sonnet. One of the things that makes Larkin's poem so powerful and moving is that while trying to resist the clichés inherent in his subject he does not disavow the emotion or feeling that has led him to them. Larkin appears to move beyond the complaint of unrequited love that Sidney pitches to underscore a condition of alienation, by now a convention of twentieth-century art. Moreover, he does this, ironically, by using personification ("The hardness and the brightness and the plain / Far-reaching singleness of that wide stare"). Larkin's poem does that most complex of tasks: it self-consciously reiterates the tradition of a poetic convention, in this case concerning the sympathetic powers of the moon; it discards the tradition, and then seemingly replaces it with something fresh and new. But how much different, really, is Larkin's "wide stare" from the "looks" and "languished grace" that Sidney assigns his moon? Not as much as the diction and tone of Larkin's poem might make it appear, for in the end Larkin reaffirms "the strength and pain / Of being young," which is also one of Sidney's poignant dilemmas.

Finally, what we see in the relationship Larkin forges with Sidney is another level of poetic complexity. In "The Flower of Coleridge," Borges traces "the history of the evolution of an idea through the heterogeneous texts of three authors" (Coleridge, H. G. Wells, and Henry James). He does this in order to explore Shelley's notion "that all the poems of the past, present, and future were episodes or fragments of a single infinite poem, written by all the poets of earth." This I suppose is the ultimate expression of poetry's complexity, that, as Emerson thought, "one person wrote all the books" or that the Babel of all books, all poems, all words, all language is the attempt to make one human utterance.

An Exact Ratio

◦◇◦

IN 1971 AS A FRESHMAN at a California college I did not want to be attending I thought my misplacement could be cured by seeking out John Berryman or Robert Lowell, two poets to whom I was devoted. By the time I got around to acting on this impulse, Berryman had committed suicide and Robert Lowell, I discovered, was living in England. My encounters with their work, however, had led me to many other poets, including William Meredith. I took notice that Berryman dedicated more "Dream Songs" to Meredith than any one else and that excerpts from Meredith's reviews of Lowell graced that poet's dust jackets. For Meredith's own *Earthwalk: New and Selected Poems,* Lowell had written: "Meredith is an expert writer and knows how to make his meters and sentences accomplish hard labors. His intelligent poems, unlike most poems, have character behind them." The photograph of Meredith from *Earthwalk* showed a man nothing like the poets I imagined I might study with. Instead of a shaggy and bearded Berryman among Irish ruins or the bushwacked countenance of Lowell in Berg's and Mezey's *Naked Poetry,* Meredith in stark contrast maintained a civic face: handsome, full, and solid.

In August of 1972, before leaving to study in England for a semester, I spent two weeks hitchhiking through New England, visiting schools I thought I might transfer to the following year. I had learned from his book-jacket that Meredith taught at Connecticut College. And so on an oppressively humid day, shortly after the massacre of the Israeli Olympic team members in

Munich, I arrived in New London. It was lunch hour when I got to the college's admissions office, where only one person was on duty. Fortunately, she had seen Meredith earlier in the day. She urged me to find him before he went home and showed me the way to Thames Hall, where the English Department was housed. I encountered Meredith negotiating a narrow back staircase. He was struggling with a standard Remington typewriter and now was forced to cradle it uncomfortably as I explained myself from a few steps below. There was no air conditioning in the building and the humidity was not only suffocating but it possessed the deep vacant emptiness of a school building in hibernation. Meredith realized soon I was a situation that couldn't be dealt with in the stairway. He suggested we talk in his office.

William Meredith was the first poet I had ever met and to find him weighted with a typewriter, his face pricked with perspiration, his manner so like the manner of other mortals I knew, startled me with familiarity and shocked me into my first glimpse of the truth that a poem or any art always begins with a particular man or woman. This particular man, William Meredith, was nothing like the person in the book-jacket portrait. He had ragged, longish gray hair, combed straight back and tucked behind his ears where it curled up from under the lobes. He had respectably fashionable sideburns. His eyes had large blue irises, the kind of blue you see in Chinese porcelain. He wore a blue, open-collar shirt and flared-bottom chinos. And his feet were bracketed by sandals. The most distinctive thing about him was his face. It was really two faces, like halves of the moon in different phases. And I wondered if he had suffered a stroke that had left one side partially paralyzed. He listened courteously to me and at one point pulled out the typing leaf from his desk on which he propped his feet.

Out of my infatuations with Berryman and Lowell, I had constructed a tenderfoot's map of contemporary American poetry. It led me by way of uncritical association to think of Meredith as a confessional poet. About this I couldn't have been more wrong. Meredith, I would discover, loved the work of Berryman and Lowell but he loved the particular men and their difficult struggles more. One of the things I would learn from Meredith was that a poet's work was not merely an expression of his experience but that it was interesting and intriguing, and necessary, to the degree in which it enacted a struggle between the private and public, the personal and impersonal. He often cited Berryman's essay "The Development of Anne Frank," and one of his favorite contemporary poems was Jack Gilbert's "The Abnormal is Not Courage." Meredith begins a memoir about W. H. Auden by quoting the poet Louis Coxe, a Princeton roommate of Meredith's, who called Auden "So public a private man."

When I started Connecticut College in the fall of 1973 Meredith was finishing the persona sequence *Hazard, the Painter*. In the most reductive terms it is an optimist's response to the dark times that yielded the suicides of Plath, Jarrell, Berryman, and Sexton and the politics of Vietnam and Watergate. In the poem, Meredith has put an alter ego, Hazard, "in charge of morale in a morbid time." In *Hazard* and the poems that were to follow, until his silencing stroke in 1983, his overriding concern is morale. In "In Loving Memory of the Late Author of Dream Songs," Meredith defined the peculiar nature of this morale and his preoccupation with it:

> Morale is what I think about all the time
> now, what hopeful men and women can say and do.
> But having to speak for you, I can't
> lie. "Let his giant faults appear, as sent
> together with his virtues down," the song says.
> It says suicide is a crime
> and that wives and children deserve better than this.
> None of us deserved, of course, you.
>
> Do we wave back now, or what do we do?
> You were never reluctant to instruct.
> I do what's in character, I look for things
> to praise on the river banks and I praise them.
> We are all relicts, of some great joy, wearing black,
> but this book is full of marvelous songs.
> Don't let us contract your dread recidivism

8

and start falling from our own iron railings.
Wave from the fat book again, make us wave back.

Morale and optimism were not fashionable notions to be touting in the seventies and early eighties, and Meredith knew it. He was acutely aware that morale and morality, praising and preaching, can be easily and even willfully confused. "Temperament" was a word he liked to use when describing the imperatives one lives by. Our temperaments were to be discovered as examples of human response. They were transcendental features of one's character. Character did not suggest balance and stability and harmony but rather the arena where the public and private parts of one's self might negotiate the terms of an existence.

I wanted the drama of Berryman and Lowell, the fire-breathingness and on-the-edgeness-of-things they represented and not the responsible struggle of Meredith's cause. Initially, it was hard for me as his student to take in what he was saying, though through the rigor and beauty, the fair arguments, enacted in his poems I could hear its frequencies. Also, the example of his generosity—his willingness to include others in many aspects of his life—was as disarming as it was instructive. Meredith himself was his own best argument for optimism and hope. In the classroom he treated all of our various motives, ambitions, and pretensions with seriousness and candor. Very little time was spent editing the stories and poems we brought to class. Meredith was more interested in approaching our work, any work, in order to get at the source of what he might call its original insight or particular response to experience. He drew on the tradition of English poetry, especially the Romantics, not in any scholarly or esoteric way but in a way that allowed us to see how we struggle to make sense of life through art. In 1983, I sat in on an interview conducted by the *Paris Review* with him. In response to a question about his relatively low output of six poems per year, he said, "I wait until the poems seem to be addressed not to 'Occupant' but to 'William Meredith.'" And he repeated a claim for poetry I remembered him making frequently when I was a student:

"Poetry and experience should have an exact ratio." As a teacher he was interested in getting his students to see that our job not just as writers but as men and women was to avoid the default status of "Occupant."

Since I was determined to become a writer and unerringly if not prematurely thought myself one, and since I had traveled physically and culturally, from California and Arizona, so far to cultivate my vocation, I was constantly crossing the threshold of his office. I know I must have been awkwardly persistent and to other students a hog for his time and attention. And since I had declared my intentions so early to Meredith, I must have assumed he knew what my expectations were, regardless of my talents. Whatever awkwardness obtained because of my urgencies, Meredith negotiated it easily and very soon had taken me on unconditionally. On a number of occasions I was invited to informal dinners at his house or to accompany him to readings at nearby Wesleyan and Yale. Once he asked me to drive him in his car to a reading at St. Michael's College in Vermont. He was serving a term as secretary for the American Academy and National Institutes of Arts and Letters and wanted to use the time in the car to work on citations for the recipients of that year's awards. We had got off to a late start but for the first couple hours I kept to the fifty-five-mile-per-hour speed limit. After all I was driving my distinguished teacher's car, a faded, hand-me-down Cadillac, a gift from his stepmother no less! At one point Meredith broke from his work, leaned over so he could see the speedometer, and then looked outside the window. With this information he calculated I would not deliver him to his reading in time. "I'll pay for the ticket," he reassured me. As the car responded to his hint, he returned calmly to his citations. But most of the times I accompanied Mr. Meredith, which is what I called him until my day of graduation when he asked me to stop, he was the chauffeur. He liked to engage whoever he was with in conversation about things they knew that he might not. I could talk about the desert. For his part he tried his best to teach me about the trees and creatures of New England. I remember learning about the delicate blossoms of the shad blow tree and how Frost had accurately portrayed the oven bird in his poem of that title.

Meredith himself had accompanied Robert Frost on Frost's last reading trip to California, in 1961. They took the train. One night several days into the journey, they quarreled. I can't remember if Frost lost his temper with Meredith, or if it was the other way around. But the upshot was that Frost was the one who tried to patch things up by telling him, "I brought you along on this trip so you could see a little how I take myself." Meredith liked to say with regard to that incident that a definition of style "is how a man takes himself." As a teacher and later as a friend what I learned most consistently from William Meredith was that he took himself both seriously and playfully. He preferred directness over coyness; self-effacement over self-aggrandizement. He was, to rephrase his poem, a relict of some great joy who refused to wear black.

During spring break of 1975, I attended a reading he gave with X. J. Kennedy at the New School. Daniel Halpern, who had arranged the reading, introduced the poets. He also informed us that Charles Wright and Mark Strand were in the audience. These were poets I was just finding my way to and was excited to see them in the flesh. After the reading Meredith suggested I come along with everyone to dinner. There were a number of other guests as well including his sister, Kay, and Grace Schulman, as well Wright, Strand, Halpern, and a staff member of Halpern's at *Antaeus*.

At dinner there was talk about Montale having recently been given the Nobel Prize for Literature. Someone reported that one of Montale's responses to the award was, "In a life of mostly unhappiness, this makes it a little less unhappy," or so I remember. Montale's words brought vocal and head-shaking approval from different parts of the table. But from Meredith there was silence, uncomfortable, ruminating silence that soon turned to argumentative disapproval. He couldn't understand what there was to praise in Montale's attitude toward the prize and life. He argued that our obligation as writers was to speak against the despair, "fashionable despair" is the phrase he used, characterized by Montale. Everyone had had a lot of wine and Meredith had been drinking vodka. There was a kind of squaring off between him and a few others, while most, after making feeble mediating gestures, remained neutral, though ill at ease. After a while there was a cessation of hostilities but even so it was difficult to continue with dinner. Meredith's quarrel, of course, wasn't with Montale or even with the people at dinner, it was with a culture that no longer valued the poet as the singer of its tribe's songs, and the realization that the values he honored were no longer prized. Nevertheless, he wasn't going to accept the shift from hope to despair that he believed had taken place all around him. A few hours earlier he had used his alter ego Hazard to state his case:

> Gnawed by a vision of rightness
> that no one else seems to see,
> what can a man do
> but bear witness?
>
> And what has he got to tell?
> Only the shaped things he's seen—
> a few things made by men
> a galaxy made well.
>
> Though more of each day is dark,
> though he's awkward at the job,
> he squeezes paint from a tube.
> Hazard is back at work.

If Frost had brought Meredith along to see how he took himself, Meredith had provided me with a similar opportunity that night. What I witnessed in Meredith's argument at dinner was how conviction can distort a man's style. The usually decorous and chivalrous citizen poet who used form and convention—social and artistic—to harness his powerful feelings and emotions allowed me to see what the feelings themselves might be like. Perhaps most of the people at the dinner thought Meredith wrongheaded and quarrelsome, but what I saw, as his student, was an act of courage. It was courage lacking finesse, perhaps, but courage nevertheless. It was a hidden aspect of Meredith's character, one that might get overlooked because of his fastidious manners. I think this courage was what Lowell saw in Meredith's poems, what was "behind them."

In 1975, I could not have known how long my association with William Meredith would last. At some point students and mentors often enact a struggle usually born of the student's need to create his own identity. But that has never happened between us. In 1983, Meredith had a stroke, when he was only sixty-four, that has left him expressive aphasic—virtually unable to speak but thoroughly capable of understanding. Although I have missed—mourned, really—the poems he has not been able to write during the last two decades, I have never been without his example of courage, in the form of his character. Character is probably even less fashionable to talk about today than it was in the seventies. When we do, we might hear it described as a form of personality infrastructure or the hard-wired components of the self. Generally, our attitude is that it's inherited or determined by the times we live in. Meredith's point, however, was that you cultivate it and use it like artistic form to resist solipsism and morbidity. Character gets tested during difficult times. In fact, that's its purpose.

I see William Meredith three or four times each year. Each time I'm in his presence I experience the original feeling of privilege I had when I first met him almost thirty years ago. Although his speaking ability is very much diminished, his spirit is as present and active as ever. He does not shy from argument, especially when he feels called to counter the dark and despairing forces of human nature. And he does not spare his former student criticism. Not too many years ago I was extolling the virtues of the English painter Francis Bacon to the painter Emily Maxwell. Meredith was in the room with us, listening intently with his handsome divided face and blue eyes. I could tell he wanted to get into the discussion but was searching for the words. Finally, they burst out of him clear and true and in character. "But so what!" he declared, "Bacon, unhappy man!"

The Truant Pen

⌒∞⌒

"LOOK IN THY HEART AND WRITE" is the direct and simplifying command the muse gives Astrophil, Sir Philip Sidney's foil, at the end of sonnet 1 in *Astrophil and Stella,* the first sonnet sequence in the English language. Critics, more than common readers, have debated whether Sidney's sonnet sequence, as well as much of his work, is merely the expression of a Renaissance courtier's wit or if Sidney is writing to a real Stella about a real love. Although both of these issues figure prominently in *Astrophil and Stella,* my interest in the sonnets has always had to do with how Sidney struggles with the influence of the past and tries to make something new of the old situation, "Loving in truth."

If we go back to Wyatt and Surrey and gaze at their sonnets, we find they possess the rough beauty and uniqueness of some very early automobiles—true horseless carriages—while in comparison Sidney's sonnets are the result of a more fully developed industry in which "the exact, regular correspondence of features of language to the same features in the metrical pattern" are brought to perfection, as John Thompson points out in *The Founding of English Metre.* In the same way that Henry Ford's production line created an automobile "industry," Sidney's understanding of the relationship of abstract pattern to the supple effects of colloquial language created a self-consciousness in him and in English poets ever since that has made language itself the underlying subject of poetry.

For Sidney "Loving in truth" is equal to, if not indivisible from, poetry and the act of writing. The long multiple clauses of the first sentence, which stretch across the octet, when reduced to its essence ("Loving in truth . . . I sought fit words") demonstrate the close connection Sidney believed existed between the experience of love and his desire to "show" its effects in language. The connection Sidney sees between love, truth, seeking, and fit words is articulated as a desire to share, with his Stella, the "pleasure of my pain."

Pleasure and pain create the emotional nexus of the sonnet and sequence. It is also the source of Sidney's argument with Petrarchan convention, in whose ideal and spiritualized love he does not believe. His difficulty in writing is linked to the difficulty he has in beatifying Stella. Dante's Beatrice might represent an abstracted form of Christian beauty but Sidney's Stella is of celestial matter, yes, but also resolutely an earthly body. Astrophil, in name, as well, shares in the celestial and corporeal attributes of his love. "Loving in truth" for Sidney means not only feeling reverence and respect for Stella but also the desire to consummate the love in a tangible way.

"Loving" and writing render Sidney, as we see in the twelfth line, "helpless," caught in the "throes" of giving birth to his poem. What causes the pain is not the verity of Sidney's love matched with Stella's laudable indifference but rather the self-consciousness Sidney experiences in trying to find "fit words" to describe the particular courtly and troubled love he possesses. Sidney's initial response to this situation is to look outward, "Studying inventions fine . . . / Oft turning others' leaves," hoping to discover in the tradition of the Italian sonnet "Some fresh and fruitful showers" to sooth his "sunburned brain." The irony of these lines tells us how empty his search really is and prepares us for the rather comical and klutzy action in the first half of the sestet, in which words halt, stay, flee, and trip over each other. Sidney transforms "others' leaves" into "others' feet," conflating the literal leaves and feet across the octet and sestet, with their metaphorical counterparts—book pages and metrical feet. The conflation is a rhetorical compression, a flourish of wit, that shows the depth of

Sidney's frustration with the Petrarchan convention. The conflict or gap Sidney discovers between the need to write about his love and the available resources of language becomes the underlying theme of the entire sonnet sequence. The high contrast of this conflict is between the heart and mind, the emotions and reason, and is delineated in the argumentative structure of the sonnet.

Before Sidney is saved by his imperative-giving muse, he finds himself cartoonishly paralyzed: "helpless in my throes, / Biting my truant pen, beating myself for spite," trapped in the very self-consciousness he knows he must avoid. By telling Sidney to "Look in thy heart and write," the muse makes it sound simple, but the conjunction that separates "heart" and "write" has rarely loomed as large. Isolated from the rest of the sonnet, this command reminds me of how Red Smith, the *New York Times* sports-writer, characterized the act of writing: "It's the easiest thing in the world to do. You just sit down at your desk and open a vein." The conflict Sidney finds himself in—between the conventions of the past and his desire to find an adequate form for his experience of love—is the basic condition all poets find themselves in each time they write. When the muse impatiently calls Astrophil a "Fool," she does so as a way of bringing the lover back to the present and his immediate concern: finding the words to express his love that will bring him the "grace" of his lover. When the muse tells Astrophil to look in his heart, she means it literally, yes, but also metaphorically, for Sidney has made his heart out of living language.

(from Astrophil and Stella)

I

Loving in truth, and fain in verse my love to show,
That she dear she might take some pleasure of my pain,
Pleasure might cause her read, reading might make her know,
Knowledge might pity win, and pity grace obtain,
I sought fit words to paint the blackest face of woe:
Studying inventions fine, her wits to entertain,
Oft turning others' leaves, to see if thence would flow

Some fresh and fruitful showers upon my sunburned brain.
But words came halting forth, wanting Invention's stay;
Invention, Nature's child, fled stepdame Study's blows;
And others' feet still seemed but strangers in my way.
Thus, great with child to speak, and helpless in my throes,
Biting my truant pen, beating myself for spite:
"Fool," said my Muse to me, "look in thy heart, and write!"

The Dog Gets to Dover

William Maxwell as a Correspondent

⁂

ONE OF THE LAST THINGS that William Maxwell wrote and published was a short essay for a Festschrift celebrating Eudora Welty's ninetieth birthday. The essay took the form of a letter. "Eudora dear," it begins, "I have been thinking how fortunate we were to have been born toward the end of the first decade of this century." What follows is a lyrical though factual list of what the America of that decade was like: "To begin with, the quiet, except on the Fourth of July. No heavy trucks, no bulldozers, no power lawnmowers. . . . The grass was full of wonderful things—spring beauties, dandelions, the one-winged seeds of the maple trees . . . sometimes a piece of tinfoil or a penny." "If there was a red light in the sky," Maxwell reminds Welty, "you picked up the telephone receiver and asked Central where the fire was and she knew."

It is fitting that one of the last pieces William Maxwell published not only recalled the period of the century in which most of his own fiction was grounded but a "letter" to a writer he befriended through his work as a fiction editor of the *New Yorker*. During his life not only did literary correspondences give him great pleasure to read but he himself was a prodigious correspondent, whether it be with family and friends or the writers he worked with during his forty years at the *New Yorker*. In the special collections of the University of Illinois–Urbana Library, Maxwell's archive of correspondence is massive and includes John Updike, Louise Bogan, John Cheever, Peter Taylor, Harold

Brodkey, Kay Boyle, John O'Hara, Irwin Shaw, Mary McCarthy, Tennessee Williams, and James Thurber, to name a few. Large portions of his letters, such as the correspondence with Robert Fitzgerald and J. D. Salinger (the latter to be kept private as both writers wished) will eventually form part of the Urbana archive. Once all of his letters reside in the Urbana archive, it will comprise one of the most significant collections of American literary correspondence of the twentieth century and is likely to demonstrate that Maxwell was one of this century's great letter writers. Not all of his letters are squirreled away in the Urbana library. Already, two collections of his correspondence have been published: *The Happiness of Getting It Down Right: Letters of Frank O'Connor and William Maxwell* (1996) and *The Element of Lavishness: Letters of Sylvia Townsend Warner and William Maxwell, 1938–1978* (published in 2001, shortly after his death). Maxwell's job as a fiction editor at the *New Yorker* put him in a unique position to foster such a wide-ranging correspondence, but this alone does not make his letters unique. What is of paramount importance in defining Maxwell's correspondence is the character of the man who wrote them and his ability to befriend and love people.

In the introduction to his collection of essays and reviews, *The Outermost Dream,* Maxwell wrote, "Diaries, memoirs, published correspondence, biography, and autobiography—which are what I was asked to consider—do not spring from prestidigitation or require a long apprenticeship. They tell what happened—what people said and did and wore and ate and hoped for and were afraid of, and in detail after often unimaginable detail they refresh our idea of existence and hold oblivion at arms length." That Maxwell was attracted to the letters of literary figures, as well as their biographies, memoirs, and journals, is made clear by the fact that he agreed only to review examples of these for the *New Yorker*. The last review essay Maxwell published with the magazine, in 1994, covered the first two volumes of *The Letters of Robert Louis Stevenson.*

Roland Barthes, in his essay "Deliberation," cites four types of motives for the keeping of a journal: poetic, historical, utopian, and amorous. The "amorous" motive constitutes the "journal as a workshop of sentences: not 'fine phrases' but of correct ones," in which language refines the "exactitude of the speech according to an enthusiasm . . . a fidelity of intention which greatly resembles passion." Letter writing, too, can take the form of a journal. Maxwell once said of his correspondence with O'Connor, "Letter writing for me was a little like keeping a journal." The "amorous," especially in its exactitude, enthusiasm, and passion, is everywhere present in the letters of William Maxwell. Writing to Sylvia Townsend Warner in April 1958, he declared, "I have often thought that we were meant for each other—you to write to me and I to read you. . . . every sentence I have ever read of yours gave me immediate intense pleasure—at the world as you saw it, and at how you said what you were saying—the intense pleasure of appreciating a personal style." Although Maxwell and Warner met only twice during their lives, they were in such constant contact through letters that Maxwell once told her, "The only person I really see a great deal of, among all my friends, is Sylvia" (April 1961).

Similar to his relationship with Sylvia Townsend Warner, Maxwell's relationship with Frank O'Connor started when he began editing the writer's stories for the *New Yorker*. In *The Happiness of Getting It Down Right*, it is easy to follow the progress of an editor working with his writer to the formation of an unshakable friendship. When Maxwell queries Frank O'Connor in 1947 about a story of his the magazine was going to publish, he addresses him as Mr. O'Connor, a formality that continues until 1954, when he begins to address him as O'Connor. This creeping intimacy affords him the opportunity to report in the same letter, "Last week end we went out to our house in the country, to see a man about digging a deeper well, and the first daffodil points were foolishly above the ground. In town it is very springlike, and deceptive. The kind of weather that leads young men (or did me) to fall in love with girls they don't marry." By 1955, they greet each other as Frank and Bill. In 1957, O'Connor, giving up his pseudonym—his real name was Michael John O'Donovan—refers to himself as Michael, and by the next year they each begin to sign off their letters with "love."

Once Maxwell had established a friendly intimacy with Warner and O'Connor, he extended and deepened the intimacy by writing to other members of their households. Eventually, he writes to Warner's lover Valentine, to Harriet (O'Connor's wife), and to O'Connor's daughter, Hallie-Og. And Emmy, Maxwell's wife, writes to them as well. The tone of the letters becomes familial, and the friendships collaborative and collective. Successes and failures, deaths and illnesses, holidays and inconsequential days, insights and perplexities are all shared as easily as breath. What's most striking is how unguarded and fresh the exchanges seem. Even so, one doesn't feel as if everything going on in their lives is discussed, but that a general stoicism, typical of Maxwell's generation, is in operation, filtering out what would be considered private and proprietary. Nevertheless, the emotion the letters convey is authentic and deep.

While the "amorous" nature of Maxwell's relationships with Warner and O'Connor is similar, the tone of the letters is markedly different. When writing Warner, Maxwell speaks from that part of himself, he once confessed to her, which as a little boy preferred the company of women. With O'Connor, he is more direct, chummy, and playfully competitive. "An egotist I certainly am," he writes to O'Connor in 1961, who was recovering from surgery on his hand, "Didn't I rush off, two days after I got your letter, and have a lump removed from my shoulder, just so you wouldn't get ahead of me." Partly what we hear is the conversation of two family men, discussing their wives and children, living arrangements, the vexation of not finding time to work, and partly we hear Maxwell playing the role of editor and nudge. "Scold, scold, scold, how boring Protestants are," he tells his friend in 1963, after urging him to sharpen the focus in a piece he is working on. While Maxwell as editor is everywhere evident in his correspondence with O'Connor ("I don't know why I badger you so much," he writes later that year), intimacy and affection break through constantly. "It's strange to think of last Sunday's sleet beating against the windows of your forsaken apartment," he writes when O'Connor is away from New York. "Do you ever think how much the objects miss you? Or how much I do?"

Maxwell was never interested in keeping a journal, though he did attempt one during his apprenticeship years. Harold, one of the protagonists in his novel *The Château,* notices that his wife is keeping a diary of their trip through France and thinks, "She had a façade that she retired behind . . . the image of an unworldly, well-bred, charming-looking, gentle young woman. The image was not even false to her character; it merely left out half of it. . . . It was the façade that was keeping the diary." Tom Mallon, in *A Book of One's Own: People and Their Diaries,* points out that diaries are the only form of writing to which the verb "keep" is applied: "One doesn't 'keep' a poem or a letter or a novel. . . . But diaries are . . . about the preservation and protection of the self." In conversation, Maxwell once told me that his disinclination for keeping a diary came from the dual tedium produced by writing to one's self and for a future, unknown reader. The necessity of having someone to whom his writing was addressed was as true for Maxwell as it was for Sylvia Townsend Warner, whom he described as needing "to write for an audience, a specific person, in order to bring out her pleasure in enchanting."

My own correspondence with William Maxwell began in 1981, after I had dinner at his East Eighty-sixth Street apartment as a guest of William Meredith, who had been my teacher in college. Several years earlier, I had been introduced to Maxwell's work when Meredith told me that he had been the ghostwriter of the jacket copy for Meredith's 1975 book of poems, *Hazard the Painter.* I was a sophomore in college then, and it was made clear to me that I was meant to keep the bones of this knowledge buried. As an acolyte to this secret, I felt as if I had an intimacy with Maxwell even before I met him.

At dinner I met his wife, Emmy, and Brookie, his daughter, who is close to my age. The evening was courteous, but what I remember most is the sincerity and intimacy the Maxwells produced by the quiet force of their presence. Sitting in their living room, we talked about poetry, mainly, and Bill would occasionally go to the bookshelf and take out Yeats or Hardy or a volume by someone else whose name came up, and we would take turns reading. This went on before and after the meal. It sounds a little like the way hymns are sung at church, but it wasn't like that at all. Reverence was not the overriding mood; it was more like a desire to put what one cares about directly into the ears of those one loves.

A few weeks later, in response to a thank-you note I had sent from California, where I was living, I received a postcard with a single sentence echoing my own pleasure with the evening. It also included their New York and Yorktown Heights telephone numbers and an invitation to call the next time I was in the city. From 1981 to 1987, we exchanged letters occasionally, perhaps four or five times a year, but after April 1987, when Bill and Emmy stayed with my wife and me in Baltimore after a reading Bill had given at the University of Maryland, where I taught, the frequency of our correspondence increased to meet the needs of a friendship that to my own bewilderment (Bill was my senior by almost fifty years) began to deepen.

Among the many remarkable things I learned about letter writing from William Maxwell during my years of corresponding with him, these stand out. No letter should ever go unanswered. Receiving a letter in which illness or personal difficulty are mentioned requires not only a response containing a remedy or solution but a follow-up phone call. Books, writing, reading, and childhood are paramount topics, followed by wives, children, and friends, and then in no particular order cats, dogs, birds, gardens, domestic arrangements, music, museums and their current exhibitions, and in general whatever else might create delight and pleasure in the reader. I was to learn that what one should live for more than anything else are small moments of overwhelming astonishment. "All pleasure," he wrote to Sylvia Townsend Warner in January 1961, "is got from the rubbing off of somebody else's pleasure in something. From eye to eye and skin to skin. A cousin of love-making."

Maxwell believed "the personal correspondence of writers feeds off left-over energy." This produces a feeling of "lavishness" because, as he noted, "the chances of any given letter's surviving is fifty-fifty at most." It also produces a feeling "of confidence—of the relaxed backhand stroke that can place the ball anywhere that it pleases the writer to have it go." Typical of the kind of lavishness he could produce is this, in a letter to Warner in September 1966: "If you are lucky, you find yourself in the field where the flower is growing. You don't buy tickets for it. Dear old, old friend, tiredness one gets over, but don't allow permanent melancholy in the house." And a typical moment of confidence, also in a letter to Warner, September 1958: "The peach tree has its first crop, of white peaches that taste like nectarines. The roses are about to bloom once more, and they'd better hurry. The cloud compositions are the best in years. And both children have had their hair cut, which always has the effect of putting them in quotation marks for a few days."

Maxwell wanted characters in fiction to sound like real people, not caricatures. As a result, snippets of conversation O'Connor might report—such as this, in a letter to Maxwell in 1958, of a woman in Dublin: "Oh, sir, I can't sleep at night with my mind"—thrilled him. Maxwell peppered his own letters with the speech and idiom of his native Midwest. To Warner he admits that phrases he heard his Aunt Edith use, such as "crazy as Dick's hatband," astonished him because their "explanation seemed over the hill of Time, beyond recovering." I remember when "crazy as Dick's hatband" showed up puzzlingly in a letter he sent to me, as well as other idioms and figures of speech. Phrases that pop up not only in my letters from Maxwell but in those he sent to Warner and O'Connor as well might include, "And I am never one to paint instead of going to my mother's funeral"; "Well, leg over leg and the dog gets to Dover"; "I will keep my eye on the cork and report any bobbing"; or "this will make [him] morbid or I don't know Arkansas." Not only do they carry an idiomatic vividness, but they are indicative of Maxwell's habit of metaphoric thinking, a habit that has its origins in the way people talked and was therefore alive in a way that was practical and useful. Whenever I came across one of these phrases in a letter, it seemed like a found poem.

Just as Nabokov liked to illustrate his lectures, Bill, who had once been an art student, might include a drawing in a letter. He once sketched a walker for Warner when old age and a fall had reduced her to hobbling. He was also an impeccable direction giver. Despite the elaborate directions he once sent me that were meant to lead me from my apartment in New Haven, Connecticut, to their country house in Westchester County, I got supremely turned around and stubbornly lost. When I finally called to get my bearings, there was not only worry in his voice but contrition for having failed me. Another time, when I arrived at their Manhattan apartment after they were in bed, and a key had been left for me with the doorman, I found this typed note on the nightstand in the guestroom: "Michael: I probably don't need to tell you, to set the alarm you turn the knob in the center of the back of the clock and push down on the bar at the back so that it rises above the level where it now is. There's fresh orange juice in the refrigerator. Sleep well."

Directions, drawings, and notes not only were the result of Bill's fastidious courtesy and manners, but revealed a selfless, worrying preoccupation with the other person. Accompanying the drawing of the walker to Warner, in a letter of February 1978, was this fretting concern: "I am haunted by the thought of you putting out your hand for a steadying piece of furniture that isn't, as it happens, there. Alas I don't think it [a walker] will do anything for the pain in your legs. Wings is [*sic*] what you really need. Why has it taken me so long to think of it?" The health and well-being of his friends were foremost, but all things being equal, he fretted over whether they were writing. In his letters to O'Connor this worry took the form of playful badgering. "The number of things," he laments in a letter of June 1963, "you can think of to do, the number of talents you can come up with, to keep from writing stories, exceeds all comprehension. . . . But where are those stories that always used to come in threes?"

His habits of paying meticulous attention to the tiniest of details—"the knob in the center of the back of the clock"—are also the extension of his writer's passion for accuracy. Nevertheless, he did not pay attention merely in order to get things right for the page. Accuracy deflected complacency. In older age these habits helped to keep him sharp and focused and engaged in life, and although he was no longer making sentences for stories, he was still writing letters to a wide range of friends. Many of them, like myself, were considerably younger, and so for us his letters contained the wisdom of Solomon spoken with the gentleness of Saint Francis. In 1994 he wrote to me, "Either you retire from life or you advance to meet it."

For Maxwell, letters were not merely a way of staying in touch with friends but a means to participate intimately in their lives. His sympathetic powers were so strong that for him reading an account of some incident, in books or letters, nearly equaled the experience itself. When the mother of Valentine Auckland, Warner's lover, died, Bill wrote to Warner in September 1961, "I loved her. That is I loved reading about her." Throughout his life, he was deeply affected by books. He read the *Goncourt Brothers Journals* a page at a time, and when he finished, he declared, in another letter to Warner, from December 1958, "All I ask of life is the privilege of being able to read." In 1996 when he was rereading Keats's letters, he had to stop because, as he wrote me, "I was not ready to let Keats die." And in another letter I received from him, he made this rapturous statement about Marianne Moore: "Reading her prose is like looking at the morning star."

Toward the end of his life, reading and writing came together in a kind of painful synesthesia. In the spring of 2000, one of his letters admitted, "I can't find anything to read that isn't overstimulating. I am about half way through *War and Peace* and if I read that after dinner I go on living it in my dreams. Awful things that I know are going to happen, scenes I have made up in my sleep and sometimes just writing." In one of the last interviews he gave, Maxwell said the only thing he would regret about no longer being alive was that he would no longer be able to read—no Chekhov, no Turgenev, no Tolstoy, no Keats.

The ability to live fully in a world created of language is one of the qualities that made him such an insightful and empowering editor. He once wrote to Warner: "It is one of the pleasures of my life, that your stories come directly from you to me. So close does it bring us that I feel as if I could reach out and take the pages as you add the last correction, bunch them together, and decide that it is safe to let go of them." In 1965, he wrote to both O'Connor and Warner about an exhibit of manuscripts by Hawthorne, Crane, Conrad, Woolf, and many others, on display at the New York Public Library. From the seeds of Virginia Woolf's sketchy "plan" of *To the Lighthouse,* Maxwell told O'Connor that he heard "the voice of the novelist talking to himself. In the midst of miracles, the future lying all clear around him, modesty struggling with pride, the work all to come, and farther away still the nagging doubts that will slow the whole thing down and spoil his pleasure after the accomplishment is in hand." The miraculous and magical work of writing was something he believed in with a quiet religiosity. He finished his letter to O'Connor this way: ". . . so it [*To the Lighthouse*] was a literary masterpiece. Though I know I shouldn't, I believe in the life everlasting, and the communion of saints, provided the saints are writers."

When writing about William Maxwell it is easy to make him sound saintly, not because he was a saint, but because his nature was so generous and his conversation and concerns were so highly attenuated—ascetic, really—on the life of art and writing, and because in spite of this asceticism, he was also very much grounded in the world of things and the details of domesticity. He was not unaware of the difficulty his preoccupations might make for those close to him and the sacrifices others were forced to make on his behalf, especially Emmy and his daughters. Nevertheless, he was unrepentant when he confronted this aspect of his life. In response to a complaint of mine about the pressures of writing and teaching, and the effect this had on my wife and sons, he wrote, "That it is not easy to be the child of a writer is something that I'm sure has crossed your mind." And then as if seeing back to a similar panorama that once occupied his own life, he continued, "The past cannot be undone, and it doesn't seem to be easy to draw a line between it and the present. If I had it to do all over again I don't suppose I would change anything. The writer in me would say, how dare you?"

The writer in Maxwell represented an unremitting and unblinking force. In his letters to me, he often focused on the rapturous aspects of the creative act, the exaltative energy that carried with it an almost moral urgency about art, and the writers who comprised his lineage—his communion of saints. But behind this, I always felt the pressure of that other, darker energy: the energy that could sometimes seduce by idealizing—"there is nothing about Keats you haven't read"—or praise by exaggeration—"The Odysseus poem is a marvel. I clasp it to me like a person. If you had written only that one poem it would get you into the company of true poets." The goal of this exuberance was not only to inspire others to work at their fullest capacity but to control and pacify through love the powerful emotions that swirled inside of him, right up to the time of his death.

Maxwell did not seek perfection either in life or work. Instead what he found to be achievable was a kind of human capaciousness that was more like a state of being. In his review of Stevenson's letters, he quotes what Hugh Walpole said of Francis Sitwell: "There is nothing you could not tell her. . . . she had to the last that certain stamp of great character, an eager acceptance of the whole life." This state of eager acceptance was one he could recognize in others as well. He described Emmy's ninety-two-year-old father to Warner, in a letter of April 1978, this way: he "has always been a good letter writer, but his letters have recently taken on a kind of radiance, as if he had stopped taking any ordinary part in life, stopped worrying, I mean, about the outcome of things, and simply looked around him with delight at the way everything is." And of a childhood neighbor he encountered on a trip to Lincoln, Illinois, while researching his memoir, *Ancestors,* he concluded that "in the razor's edge between living and dying herself, she has come to regard everything and everybody as beautiful and miraculous. As indeed they are." Most of my own friendship with Maxwell took place during his ninth and tenth decades and as a result I can attest to the fact that he had reached a state of marvelous regard for the world. In one of the last letters I received from him, he came to this realization while watching his grandson, Ellis, play in the park: "I was struck by the fact that he didn't express his happiness merely by the look on his face but with his whole body—legs, everything."

Maxwell has been criticized at times for the overly fastidiousness of his life and art. The source of this criticism promotes a fallacy about art, especially twentieth-century art. In part this fallacy says that inner turmoil needs to express itself in external turmoil: manic art equals manic life or vice versa. Or that controlled and orderly surfaces are repressive and untruthful. Maxwell's approach, one consistent with his temperament, was different. He developed a manner of working that allowed him to lock onto a particular frequency of experience and to sharpen the tuning as finely as possible. The result was clarity and definition. Background noise and static were filtered out by his sensibility, which was as acute as Flaubert's and as economical as Chekhov's. The clarity could be as explicit as his memory of the decade he and Eudora Welty were born into, or it could be excruciating. The last time I spoke with Bill was the morning after Emmy died. "There's been a failure in the arrangements," he said. "Harriet is coming this morning to take Emmy to the incinerator, and instead of bringing one body, she should be bringing two." He also told me that while sitting with Emmy, after she had died, he remembered that shortly after his mother's death, more than eighty years before, a man his father did not like for some reason had come to pay his respects at their house. When his father saw who it was, he slammed the door in the man's face. Bill was standing near his father at the time. He told me that he didn't realize anyone, let alone his father, could treat others that way. But what was most vivid about the incident, and what he saw there in the darkness as he sat with Emmy, was snow falling on the man his father had turned away. Later I thought of something he had written to me a few months earlier, in what turned out to be the last letter I received from him: "God knows there's much to grieve over and only a general agreement that we must get on with it prevents us from giving ourselves over to sorrow. And to joy."

Becoming a Reader,
Becoming a Writer

I'VE WANTED TO BE A WRITER since I was seventeen. That's when I had to read a novel a week for a high-school senior English class. At some point that year it occurred to me that if I could put together enough words to fill a book, the way the authors I had been reading had, it would be an achievement all at once impossible to do but immeasurably worthwhile. I didn't have in mind a story I wanted to tell nor did I have an upwelling of emotion I wanted to channel. My inspiration, if that's what it was, was a simple challenge. During the summer of my senior year, with a typewriter my mother had gotten wholesale from an uncle in the typewriter business and given to me as a graduation gift, I spent every morning filling up sheets of paper with words before heading off to my job as a lifeguard. At the end of the summer I had more than a hundred pages filled with incoherent language. I would call it stream of consciousness if at the time I had possessed a consciousness, but I didn't. All I possessed was energy of a sort and a workman-like desire to stay on task. I was like someone who wanted to build a house but without plans or experience could only figure out how to chop down the trees that might eventually be milled for lumber. But I didn't know this at the time. I thought I was constructing a palace.

My plan for writing made me a lousy lifeguard. I had been hired to watch a pool at a large apartment complex in Phoenix, Arizona, where I lived. But while on duty I mainly read books, sometimes two or more a day, sitting in a webbed chair beneath an umbrella at a table near the edge of the pool.

What I was doing reading Balzac's *The Fatal Skin,* I don't know, but while I was in the middle of what the book jacket touted "the best introduction to the immense and bewildering Balzacian universe," I heard a scream, and then, "She's drowning, she's drowning!" And there in the water was a girl, face-down, like a jellyfish with arms. When I got to her and turned her over, her eyes were closed and I couldn't tell if she was breathing. The woman who had been screaming was now yelling, "She's blue, she's blue!" Then miraculously the girl opened her eyes. She wasn't blue. She was breathing fine. But the yelling woman, the others crowding around the pool, and my hand that gripped her shoulder like a gaff hook, terrified her into tears. Then a woman, her mother, waded into the water, gathered her into her arms and stifled the sobbing. I followed in their wake to the shallow end where they sat for several minutes before the mother led her daughter to their apartment.

The Fatal Skin got slipped under my towel and I sat attentively the rest of the day, feeling terrible and guilty. I figured once word about the result of my inattentiveness got around to the apartment managers I'd be fired. Instead the mother of the girl returned in the afternoon and thanked me for saving her daughter. The mother confessed that it was her fault. She should have been watching her daughter more closely. At the time, of course, I didn't understand there was no justice in the world. I thought the guilty were punished and the virtuous rewarded. I had been taught to stand up and take whatever came to me as a result of my own actions. But I didn't know how to take what I didn't deserve. And what I didn't deserve, I was pretty sure, was to be thanked. I'd like to say that I learned my lesson and spent the rest of the summer reading only when I was in the safety of my parents' house. But the truth is I continued to read on the job, though in an importantly different way. What this experience forced on me was a habit of always being called back to the world, to be constantly looking up from the page, whether of reading or of writing, simply, to check on the world. Sometimes I am so beguiled and distracted by what I see that I lose touch with the words I am attending to. Sometimes what I see frightens me and I return to that land of a different making. For me, the tension between these two realms produces whatever accuracy of attention might occasionally rise in my work. In this going back and forth between the imagination and what appears to be the physical world, language as the translating or transforming medium carries me.

In the many different rooms I have set up shop as a writer, in the past twenty-five years, I have always, whenever I could, stationed my writing desk near a window. The necessary lesson I learned the summer of my goal-oriented inspiration to be a writer was never lose contact with the world.

Sometimes I tell myself the drowning girl was merely relaxing, floating the dead man's float. At other times I tell myself if I hadn't gotten to her when I did she might have drowned for real. The greater lesson of that summer, I can see now, is that either version of the experience could be true and that a writer learns to be faithful to both.

State Flower, Poet Laureate,
State Song

⌒∞⌒

WHEN EBENEZER COOKE hands a letter of introduction to Lord Baltimore in John Barth's historical farce *The Sot-Weed Factor,* the nobleman, seeing that it's signed *Ebenezer Cooke, Poet,* asks, "What might that mean, pray? Can it be you earn your bread by versifying? Or you're a kind of minstrel, belike that wanders about the countryside, a-begging and reciting? 'Tis a trade I know little of, I confess't." And Cooke responds, "Poet I am, . . . and no mean one may it be; but not a penny have I earned by't, nor will I ever. The muse loves him who courts her for herself alone, and scorns the man who'd pimp her for his purse's sake."

Cooke proposes to Lord Baltimore that the governor of the province employ him as its "Poet and Laureate." His ambition he declares will be to write the *Marylandiad,* "an epic to out-epic epics: the history of the princely house of Charles Calvert, Lord Baltimore and Lord Proprietor of the Province of Maryland, relating to the heroic founding of that province! The courage and perseverance of her settlers in battling barb'rous nature and fearsome salvage to wrest a territory from the wild and transform it to an earthly paradise!"

In April of 2001, when I raised my right hand in an ornate reception room of the State House in Annapolis and swore to carry out the duties of poet laureate of the State of Maryland as set down by statutes governing the position, I was at once terrified at the formality of the ceremony and delighted to think that I was following in the shoes of the historical Ebenezer Cooke who was the author of *The Sotweed Factor or A Voyage to Maryland, A Satyr,* 1708. I was also thinking I better get my hands on a copy of the statutes I had just sworn to uphold.

Perhaps it's because the tradition—real or not—of poet laureate in Maryland extends back before the Revolution that I did not wonder for long what its poet laureate does or perhaps because the state is small and its citizens are well-educated and curious and accepting of odd things. But more likely, it's because the modern position of its poet laureate, which was enacted into law in 1959, has been defined by four distinguished and extremely generous poets who preceded me: Lucille Clifton, Reed Whittemore, Linda Pastan, and Roland Flint. Each of these poets made many visits to schools and community groups, presided as judges for local literary contests, advised arts and education panels, and as far as I know were never asked nor volunteered to write an epic to out-epic epics.

When I looked into what my oath bound me to I found that the State of Maryland's Acts of 1959, Chapter 178, *Annotated Code,* Section 13–306, allows for the governor to "designate a citizen of the State as its laureate." It says as well that the poet laureate may not receive compensation but can be reimbursed for any expenses incurred in the performance of his duties, up to one thousand dollars for any fiscal year. The money for this is taken from the Emergency Fund of the Board of Public Works. I also discovered that Section 13–306 is a subsection of Title 13, "Emblems and Commemorative Days," which lists the state flag, seal, and a catalog of other official state things such as the state insect, fossil, crustacean, reptile, and dinosaur. Poet laureate 13–306 is sandwiched, so to speak, between the state flower (the black-eyed susan) and the state song ("Maryland, My Maryland!"). The designation comes with no proscribed duties. My oath however real can never be broken.

In Maryland the poet laureate is supported by the staff members of the Governor's Office for Special Projects. Although I have never figured out the entire range of this office's responsibilities one of the things it does, with style and efficiency, is to coordinate the state's arts education activities. The staff has worked with most of the former laureates of Maryland and because of this they possess a historical memory of the position that is extremely useful. When a new laureate needs to be appointed they help put together an informal selection committee that makes a recommendation to the governor and then the governor makes the appointment. The poet laureate of Maryland serves at the pleasure of the governor. There is no set term, though an average of four years is typical. And as the state's Annotated Code sets down, there is no stipend but expenses are reimbursed. Mindful of this lack, the Special Projects Office staff urges its poet to claim what he's owed.

Near the end of a call I received from the director of Special Projects welcoming me to the laureateship, I was asked what plans I had for my tenure. Having known my immediate predecessors and having known what sorts of duties they had performed I thought I would merely do more or less what they had done. It was clear from the director's question that I was meant to come up with a plan of my own. After thinking about it for a day or two, I decided simply to make public libraries and, if it didn't confuse the issue, community colleges, the focus of my tenure. From my experience, Maryland community colleges and public libraries rarely offered literary programs. Yet both are perhaps the most democratic institutions in the country and the range of services they provide is remarkable if not largely unheralded. Additionally, libraries and their librarians for decades have been battling, sometimes alone, to protect privacy, access to information, and free speech.

For the first twelve months after my appointment I received by phone, mail, and e-mail a steady though not overwhelming stream of invitations to participate in various kinds of literary arts endeavors. Some of these I scheduled and with others I turned to the Special Projects Office for assistance. I visited many libraries and colleges, but just as many schools and community groups, including a Rotary Club breakfast meeting, a Catholic Worker home, senior centers, and museums. It has been clear from the very beginning that these requests and invitations had very little to do with me and everything to do with the figurehead nature of the appointment. It has not only been a lesson for me in what adheres to the symbols of public life but it has been an indication of the desire that people have to hear poetry, to learn about it, and to see what it is a poet does. People have a deep need for encounters with language that exceed their normal daily encounters. And these, they rightly believe, are apt to be found in poetry. Poetry, as Philip Larkin might have it, feeds our "hunger . . . to be more serious." Not long ago at a Saturday luncheon meeting for a county friends of library group, a well-dressed man, whom I later found out was a retired architect, asked me, clearly disappointed in what I had already read, if I didn't have something darker to read. I obliged him with a poem about a childhood neighbor of mine who shot his wife and then tried, with mixed results, to shoot himself in the mouth. "Dark enough?" I asked afterward, but I couldn't tell.

I'm certain that one of the reasons I have been kept so busy as a poet laureate has been the attention that the United States laureates, from Rita Dove to Billy Collins, have brought to their positions. I suspect the notion that I should come up with a special project was related not only to the previous traditions of Maryland laureates but also because of the ambitious plans these U.S. laureates have undertaken. Robert Pinsky's "Favorite Poem Project" has been tremendously important not so much for popularizing poetry as for demonstrating that for many people poetry is already popular, although the reasons for this are mostly intimate and personal and have very little to do with notions of aesthetics. At this level poems quite often fulfill the function that prayer and meditation fulfill and they can acknowledge intense and confusing feelings while at the same time providing the consolation that inheres in the communal aspects of language. This has been an important thing to reaffirm at the beginning of a new millennium in a culture where language is used almost exclusively for inauthentic means.

Overall I believe national and state poet laureates are a positive force for poetry in the United States. They can counter some of the criticism that poetry suffers for being overspecialized and help bring poetry out of the ivory and virtual towers in which it is perceived to be hiding. An interesting tension has been created between the democratic and educative role a poet laureate is asked to play and the status bestowed on poetry through the laureate's position. One danger of relegating poetry to the status of a national or local figurehead is that it then allows poetry to be distributed like any other cultural commodity that flows through the pipeline of arts outreach. This danger is worth it and can be countered if poets talk as directly as possible to people about poetry, its history and various traditions and uses, and to challenge their notions concerning it, while upholding the mystery and strangeness that stands behind it.

For my own part I have been grateful for the honor to act as Maryland's representative of poetry to its citizens. Poetry in its effects can be subversive of the status quo and it is a rare opportunity to challenge the status quo through a public position. Nevertheless, I am always mindful, as Barth tells us Ebenezer Cooke was, that "the muse loves him who courts her for herself alone," and so I am frequently at odds with my oath to fulfill the duties of poet laureate of the State of Maryland, such as they are, and my impulse to stay put and write and let the public discourse about poetry take care of itself.

The Look of Things

The seventy-fifth anniversary of the Bread Loaf Writers' Conference began with a general welcoming of the participants and then an introduction of Middlebury College president John McCardell, who read Vermont governor Howard Dean's proclamation that Sunday, August 20, 2000 was Bread Loaf Writers' Conference Day, after which, I delivered the following informal remarks.

IT BEARS REPEATING: It's a pleasure to welcome all of you to the seventy-fifth annual session of the Bread Loaf Writers' Conference. We will continue to celebrate the anniversary with a few special events such as President McCardell's reading of the governor's proclamation, and we even have a souvenir for everyone, suitable for framing, a broadside of Robert Frost's "Hilla Spring." But while these particular occasions and remembrances will help recall the distinguished past of the conference and the role it has played in twentieth-century American letters, I believe the way we best honor the tradition is by paying attention to the present. And so to this end, we will not veer from our usual unrelenting program of lectures, workshops, classes, readings, presentations, and conferences. In other words, we will not be distracted from the work at hand.

Having said this, I realize it's appropriate to say something about the genesis of the conference—appropriate as well as making propitiatory gesture toward one of the conference founders,

Robert Frost. Robert Frost, as you probably know, lived nearby for many years and was associated with what goes on here at the end of August. For more than thirty years he could be counted on to read, lecture, play softball, and, as king of this mountain, hold a watchful and vigilant court. When Archibald MacLeish visited in 1938 Frost set fire to wads of paper at the back of this theater in an attempt to bring MacLeish's reading to a smoky panicky close. To get a good sense of who Frost was I hope as many of you as possible are able to visit Frost's cabin, which is not too far from here. There is nothing quaint or romantic about it. It was a carapace for the dark inner afflictions he kept and did not keep at bay. A visit will make clear what a profound triumph over his dark nature the poems represent.

The important thing to remember about Frost as a founder of Bread Loaf is this: He understood how necessary it was for writers at some point to make contact with other writers. And he had a simple but rather profound notion of what kind of relationships were possible between seasoned and aspiring writers. Frost in describing the ideal Bread Loaf teacher said, "He [the teacher] would turn from correcting grammar in red ink to matching experience in black ink, experience of life and experience of art." And: "He will invade them to show them how much more they contain than they can write down; to show their subject matter is where they came from." Finally, "The writer's whole nature must be in every piece he sets his hand to and his whole nature includes his belief in the real value the writing will have when finished." These ideas were sketched out in a letter Frost wrote in 1922 to George Whicher, an English professor at Middlebury College and an early biographer of Emily Dickinson, when plans were being formulated for a writers' conference, and I believe they still represent what the conference stands for.

Throughout the next eleven days, all of us will learn many useful things about the craft of writing and our meetings with editors and publishers are sure to be enlightening, but what is likely to be more important is how we become awakened to or reacquainted with the experience, as Frost saw it, that we contain more than we can write down, that we write because our "whole nature" is a baffling territory which we can only begin to explore by way of language. This awakening to the possibilities of what it means to write, and to continue to write, is the great gift Bread Loaf has given to thousands of participants. This gift sustains us when we return to the improbable and exhausting work of putting words down on the page.

During my first session as director, six years ago, William Maxwell and his wife, Emmy, visited. Before Maxwell read one of his brilliant and elegant stories from this podium, he said that Bread Loaf felt like paradise. A few weeks ago, Maxwell died at the age of ninety-one. Before closing my remarks I would like to read an excerpt from the preface to his collected stories, *All the Days and Nights*. As writers we all construct myths about how we got started and this is a portion of Maxwell's:

> The four-masted schooner lay at anchor in Gravesend Bay, not far from Coney Island. It belonged to J.P. Morgan, and I persuaded a man with a rowboat to take me out to it. In my coat pocket was a letter of introduction to the captain. The year was 1933, and I was twenty-five. I had started to become an English professor and changed my mind, and I had written a novel, as yet unpublished. I meant to go to sea, so that I would have something to write about. And because I was under the impression, gathered from the dust-jacket copy of various best-sellers, that it was something a writer did before he settled down and devoted his life to writing. While the captain was reading my letter I looked around. The crew consisted of one sailor, chipping rust, with a police dog at his side. It turned out that the schooner had been there for four years because Mr. Morgan couldn't afford to use it. The captain was tired of doing nothing and was expecting a replacement the next day and was therefore not in a position to take me on. He had no idea of when the beautiful tall-masted ship would leave its berth. And I had no idea that three-quarters of the material I would need for the rest of my writing life was already at my disposal. My father and mother. My brothers. The cast of larger-than-life-size characters—affectionate aunts, friends of the

family neighbors white and black—that I was presented with when I came into the world. The look of things. The weather. Men and women long at rest in the cemetery but vividly remembered. The Natural History of home: the suede glove on the front-hall table, the unfinished game of solitaire, the oriole's nest suspended from the tip of the outermost branch of the elm tree, dandelions in the grass. All there, waiting for me to learn my trade . . .

Before Maxwell had himself rowed out to J. P. Morgan's yacht he'd already spent considerable time perfecting his craft and had confronted the typical obstacles, trials, and doubts—the unpublished novel, the decision to reject a conventional profession—and he felt ill-equipped experientially to be a writer. That preface was written in 1995 when William Maxwell was eighty-five. The anecdote about himself and his search for the right kind of writer's experience is vividly told—the twenty-five-year-old Maxwell on the very deck of his future and yet the yacht won't sail because one of the richest men in the world cannot afford to keep it in service. With his destiny thwarted Maxwell has to spend the rest of his life writing about what he already knows—"the look of things."

Although Bread Loaf is nothing like going out to sea, it does represent for most of us the risk of a particular kind of adventure—an experience that will influence, perhaps in a profound way—the direction of our lives as writers. Each of us has our own reasons and expectations for attending the conference. As the conference director, my hope for everyone is that somehow these expectations are fulfilled but even more than the fulfillment of those expectations, I hope for the awakening or reawakening to what it is that comprises the natural history of our lives, a coming to terms with what has been calling us slyly and ineluctably to set down in words the look of things. Coming to terms with ourselves in this fashion is apt to sustain and encourage us when the conference is finished and the words that have been said here about writing become less distinct, and what we find won't blur is the suede glove or some other object waiting to be irradiated by our attention.

A Final Antidote

༺✸༻

IN 1930, AT THE AGE OF THIRTY-TWO, and in response to an increasing depression that would eventually result in hospitalizations in 1931 and 1933, Louise Bogan, who had long been in the habit of keeping a journal, began using it for a new purpose. Describing the impetus for this change, her biographer, Elizabeth Frank, has written that Bogan "recognized that she was in the grip of an emotional and creative crisis, and, despising passivity, felt that the task ahead was nothing less than total artistic and psychic reconstruction. First and most important, she would teach herself to write all over again." Not having been introduced to Rilke's poems yet, for that influential encounter was still almost five years away, Bogan would not have known how much her own reconstruction would resemble his when he came under the influence of Rodin and set out deliberately to move away from the highly wrought romanticism and allegorical density of his early poems, to making poems out of careful and scrupulous observations of the immediate world, resulting in the *New Poems,* in 1907 and 1908.

During the 1920s Bogan had kept a journal but it had been destroyed, along with most of her other papers and letters from this period, in a fire that leveled the country house she shared with her second husband, the writer Raymond Holden. This early journal however was of a different sort than the one born of her depression. Bogan's description of it indicates what she felt she lacked as a poet and writer at the time and what she hoped her new journal might lead her to. Bogan writes, "The diary kept in

Vienna in 1922 was without any real descriptive power. Then, I could only describe through a set of symbols—poetically, lyrically. Straight rendering completely baffled me; I remember this. So inner, so baffled, so *battered*—even at 24—that I noticed practically nothing; or if I did notice it, I could not put it down (in prose) with any directness."

In teaching herself directness of style, or "straight rendering" as she called it, Bogan hoped to find "the awkwardness of maturity and truth, in a style as hard as a brick." The language of symbolism, which she referred to as "the language of dream," was a mode she no longer wanted to employ. It had cut her off from the difficult truth of her experience and permitted her to live on the fierce energy of her talent and ambition, but at the age of thirty-two, she found herself feeling dead and empty. Her reinvention began in simplicity: "I saw the clear afternoon, casting the shadows of chairs one way in the room, so that the season was as clear within a house as out of doors. The shadows had the time of day written into them, as well as the look of autumn."

After a year of forcing herself to pay attention to the ordinary things around her, Bogan felt she had made good progress on her reconstruction. "I cannot yet put down all the truth as I see it," she writes, "but I shall train myself and sometimes this thing will come out truly, in detail, alive possessed, understood, first; thereafter written out. My own angers, my own despairs, therefore—and all the matters before which I now fall silent."

In this self-appraisal we hear a confidence of accomplishment that will rise and fall over the decades. In order to restore her belief in herself as a writer and to help her pass through the "dead areas" of work and feeling, Bogan will continue to seek out the unobserved space her journal offers. In a 1953 journal entry, twenty-five years after her initial "reconstruction," she reconfirms her commitment to the power and necessity of "straight rendering." Bogan writes, "And I think the only thing to do, in these dead areas, is to put down something that one has *noticed*, and not experienced actually. A bird's-eye or mouse-eye view. Told with the most careful detail and feeling for truth. Then the truth will be bearable, because the truth always comes out quite queer. It sounds so distorted and improbable that the writer's interest is kept, in spite of himself . . ."

The personal crisis that Bogan experienced in the early thirties was not only precipitated by her tumultuous marriage with Raymond Holden and her own inclination toward suspicion and paranoia, but it was also a crisis over how to come to grips with a traumatic childhood that she had long kept hidden. Elizabeth Frank saw Bogan's situation this way: "For a long time she had looked at herself and seen an intoxicating portrait of a precocious, gifted, and beautiful young woman, a reckless bohemian and inspired seeker of art and freedom." This self-image would crack under the strain of a dissolving marriage and its aftermath and while Bogan was not able to keep herself from a physical and mental collapse, she was able to retrain herself as a writer. As a result, when she was released from the hospital, she had a new method of working to fall back upon.

Along with the journal Bogan worked on during the 1930s, she started reviewing poetry for the *New Yorker,* a job she would hold for thirty-eight years. These activities didn't completely answer all of her artistic and intellectual needs and so about the same time, she began earnestly to write short stories. Between June and December of 1931, she published five of these in the *New Yorker.* Using her recently developed style of observation in these stories, Bogan began exploring events and details from her past, but she still found it difficult to openly approach the events and incidents that most profoundly affected her. In her journal of August 1932, she notes, "The continuous turmoil in a disastrous childhood makes one so tired that 'Rest' becomes a word forever said by the self to the self. The incidents are so vivid and so terrible that to remember them is inadequate: they must be forgotten." And yet memory is the very thing she can't deflect and she soon undertakes the torturous process of writing a memoir, "Journey Around My Room," which takes as its starting point the very room Bogan was living in at the time at 306 Lexington Avenue.

The memoir, which owes its imaginative framework to Xavier

de Maistre's *Voyage autour de ma chambre,* begins with a paragraph inviting the "traveler" to start the journey from the "most advantageous point" of the room, which is the bed; at the most advantageous time(s), which is midnight with moonlight lying "upon the floor," or in the early morning whose "bleak opacity . . . serves the traveler . . . as sun brightens the brick wall of the house across the yard, and sheds a feeble reflected glow upon all the objects which I shall presently name." Nevertheless, Bogan delays naming the objects in order to locate the room in relationship to the rest of the apartment, the apartment in relationship to the building, and then the building in relationship to Lexington Avenue and the Empire State Building. Once the points of the compass are taken care of, and yet still from the most advantageous point of the room, the bed, she describes the architectural features of the walls, floor, ceiling, fireplace, and the mantelpiece which bears the first solid objects: a Japanese print hanging above a group of seashells.

The print depicts "Russian sailors afflicted by an angry ocean, searchlights, a burning ship, and a boat-load of raging Japanese." This image of violence and catastrophe causes Bogan to pause and make an authorial intrusion, and as if to let herself consider her own reason for taking the journey, she remarks, "The initial mystery that attends any journey is: how did the traveler reach his starting point in the first place? How did I reach the window, the walls, the fireplace, the room itself; how do I happen to be beneath this ceiling and above this floor?" She responds with an irony and exaggeration that matches the drama of the Japanese print: "Oh, this is a matter for conjecture, for argument pro and con, for research, supposition, dialectic!" As she makes fun of the impenetrability of her own ontological processes and shows herself to be much less prepared than Livingstone ("on the verge of darkest Africa") to find her way, "some step," "some reasonable explanation for my presence here," she comes to this memory from her childhood: "One morning in March, in the year 1909, my father opened the storm door leading from the kitchen to the backstep, on Chestnut Street, in Ballardvale, a small town in Massachusetts, on the Boston & Maine Railroad . . ."

With the discovery of this memory, although she is still securely "moored" to her bed, she exits the light-softened dimension of her room to enter what has been the sealed-off universe of her past. The memory of her father opening the door is so vivid and the locating details of street, town, and railroad so specific that Bogan seems to be embarking on a journey every bit as real as Dante's, which is the literal journey of the mind's eye.

The importance of this memory is that it takes place on the day Bogan leaves Ballardvale, the third and perhaps most important of her childhood homes, with her family to start a new life in Boston. The memory ends when "the conductor lifts [her] up to the step" of the train car and at the same time she returns to the survey of her room, a survey that is now palpably different, more descriptively minute and intense. She lists the titles of books on the bookshelf, the contents of an armoire, the folds of the sheets and pillowcases. We move with Bogan through her room until she returns to the point she started from, the memory of leaving Ballardvale, which she called the "invariably" occurring "catastrophe of the journey."

Located in a dream, the catastrophe manifests itself more fully in the sound of Ballardvale's mill, and the "mill dam, fuming with water against the air, and . . . the rapids at its foot that I must gauge and dare and swim." "O Death, O Fear!" she exclaims, "The universe swings up against my sight, the universe fallen into and bearing with the mill stream." In her dream, Bogan witnesses as all of the objects in her room swirl around and are swallowed up by the turbulent water, as if they were caught up in a battle as real as the one depicted in the Japanese print. At the end of the memoir, she comes to the see that "all of these objects, provisional at best, now equally lost, rock down to translucent depths below fear, an Atlantis in little, under the mill stream (last seen through the steam from the Boston train in March, 1909)."

"Journey Around My Room" is the first of three short autobiographical pieces which she wrote for the *New Yorker* between January 1933 and October 1934 and as such it marked the beginning of a project Bogan hoped to complete but never did. The writing of these pieces must have come at a great cost to her psyche. During the composition of "Journey Around My Room," she sent several letters to Katharine White, at the *New Yorker*, apologizing for the tardiness of the memoir. That Bogan borrowed de Maistre's elaborate and imaginative conceit is an indication that at least initially she needed to find an indirect way of approaching such difficult and painful material from her past. The past represented "death" and "fear" and "catastrophe," and because these things "invariably occur," for her they carried the force of fate.

Although Bogan emerged from her depression of 1930, her recovery was incomplete. The fact that she had acquired the artistic tools to "put down all the truth" as she saw it, did not give her the emotional or physical stamina to keep the darkness at bay. After the hospitalizations of 1931 and 1933, she realized that her journey toward recovery was one she would have to take by herself and it required leaving Raymond Holden. The disruption caused by her separation and divorce from Holden brought the writing of the memoir to a halt. The last piece of autobiographical prose she worked on was the story "Letdown," published in the *New Yorker* in 1934. She would not return to her memoir until June 1953 and when she did, she again approached it in an indirect fashion by working on it a piece at a time, event by event. Many years earlier, Bogan had concluded that she was no longer a practicing poet, that poems came to her seldomly and mostly all at once, as gifts, though it wasn't as if she didn't have something to say or the desire to say it.

Similar to her dilemma of the early thirties when she needed to reconstruct her life and art, Bogan in the fifties found she needed to write toward the most important, destructive, and cruelest scenes of her life. She felt that her poems had absorbed the crucial essence of these scenes through the process of repression. In a journal entry from the sixties, she writes, "The poet represses the outright narrative of his life" and as such "absorbs it, along with life itself. The repressed becomes the poem." She finishes this idea by saying, "Actually, I have written down my experience in closest detail. But the rough and vulgar facts are not there."

Part of the reason the outright narrative must be repressed is that it is often made of details that are only half understood, distorted by the distance of years. In her memoir "Dove and Serpent," she recalls overhearing a vile and ugly neighbor named Old Jack Leonard tell her mother, "We must be wise. We must be wise as the serpent and as gentle as the dove. As the serpent, as the dove." Bogan's final paragraph of that memoir reads: "These words now lie in my memory as inexplicable . . . I did not know what they meant then, and I do not know what they mean now. It is such memories, compounded of bewilderment and ignorance and fear, that we must always keep in our hearts. We can never forget them because we cannot understand them, and because they are of no use."

In her journal of June 10, 1959, she writes, "The child lives in a region it knows nothing about. So that whatever memory of childhood remains is stable and perfect. It cannot be judged and it can never disappear. Memory has it inexplicably, and will have it forever. These things have been actually 'learned by heart.' Perhaps one of the reasons why I hesitate to write of it is that in writing I feel I shall lose it forever . . ."

But it is not simply a fear of the imperfect memory or fear of losing what she calls the quotidian essence of a scene by writing it down, that makes her hesitate. Bogan also believes that the facts are made vulgar by self-pity and remorse, and by bitterness and sentimentality coloring the event. The difficulty here is that an event may well be too awful, too terrible to approach in any manner, or any conceivable manner, and that it is only by traveling a long and torturous path that we are brought to it.

It is just such an event that Bogan wishes to explore in the fifties when she refers to her journal as "this 'long prose thing,'" which she hoped would restore her to "pure writing . . . to the capable and free setting down of 'memory and desire' . . . of what I have become and what I know.—It has been so hard for me 'to make a full breast.' . . . perhaps by spring, I can square up to the task, instead of writing cross-handed, as it were, and cross-seated, at a table . . ."

The hope that she can "square up to the task" and freely "set down . . . what I have become and what I know" is typical of the self-determination Bogan believed was necessary in order to change her art and life, as if it was merely the lack of will or strength that would prevent her. Throughout her journals, Bogan used this kind of ruthless optimism to cajole herself into action and to establish distance between herself and the chaotic emotions she experienced. She had survived severe episodes of depression in the thirties and overcome the turmoil and deprivations caused by her childhood. These victories she attributed partially to her writing, which she called a "life-saving process."

One of the recurring themes in the journals that begin in the fifties is her triumph in outlasting the dreary "old brick hotels and brownstone lodging houses" of her childhood, those places where she had always feared her life would end. In one of her journals from the fifties, she writes, "I used to think that my life would be a journey from the particular squalor which characterized the world of my childhood to another squalor, less clear in my mind, but nevertheless fairly particularized in my imagination." These places with "a milk bottle and a brown paper bag on nearly every windowsill" and "the light of a gas mantle making their dark green and brown interiors even more hideous with the melancholy of their torn and dirty laced-curtained windows intact" were the very image of failure and death for Bogan. She succeeded in avoiding them (although once in the thirties she was evicted from her apartment), but nevertheless, they still haunted and threatened her, and rightly so for they were the stages for the cruelest and most violent memories of her childhood.

The disturbing power of her later journals derives from the anguishing fact that while Bogan had managed to escape the material poverty of her past, she could not outrun the psychological and emotional damages that lay behind it. The lessening of the literal fear of these places only made the internal fears and apprehensions more forceful and prevalent. The force of these came at a time in Bogan's life when she felt her physical stamina waning and her artistic energies declining.

When Bogan comes back to her journal in the fifties, after a twenty-year hiatus, she does so by acknowledging the lateness of the hour as expressed in this passage written June 26, 1953:

> The best time to write about one's childhood is in the early thirties, when the contrast between early forced passivity and later freedom is marked; and when one's energy is in full flood. Later, not only have the juices dried up, and the energy ceased to be abundant, but the retracing of the scene of earliest youth has become a task filled with boredom and dismay. The figures that surrounded one have now turned their full face toward us; we understand them perhaps still partially, but we know them only too well. They have ceased to be background to our own terribly important selves; they have irremediably taken on the look of figures in a tragi-comedy; for we know their end, although they themselves do not yet know it. And now—in the middle-fifties—we have traced and retraced their tragedy so often that, in spite of the understanding we have, it bores and offends us. There is a final antidote we must learn: to love and forgive them. This attitude comes hard and must be reached with anguish. For if one is to deal with people in the past—of one's past—at all, one must feel neither anger nor bitterness. We are not here to expose each other, like journalists writing gossip, or children blaming others for their own bad behavior. And open confession, for certain temperaments (certainly my own), is not good for the soul, in any direct way. To confess is to ask for pardon; and the whole confusing process brings out too much self-pity and too many small emotions in general. For people like myself to look back is a task. It is like re-entering a trap, or a labyrinth, from which one has only too lately, and too narrowly, escaped.

This passage helps to illuminate why Bogan had such a difficult time finishing her memoir. While Bogan's mistrust of memory makes her ambivalent toward it, she nevertheless recognizes that particular memories "can never be forgotten." The constant encounter with them, however, does not lead to a resolution or understanding about what they represent to her. In "Dove and Serpent," when she says that memories "are of no use," she means not that they are useless and unproductive but that they are no use in solving the mysteries and enigmas of the past and they don't effect the reconciliation they are seemingly meant to achieve.

At the same time Bogan was coming to accept the limits of memory, she was also coming to understand that her own physical and artistic energies were weakening. What moved me most when I first read her journals almost thirty years ago was the terror that filled Bogan as she contemplated the waning of her powers and the courageous but hopeless way she tried to keep the terror at bay. On September 21, 1961, she writes, "It is too late to either pour it out or to reconstruct it [the past], bit by bit. What mattered got into the poems. Except for one or two *stories,* which I may be able to tell, it is all there. With the self-pity left out . . . And the poems depended on the *ability* to love (Yeats kept saying this, to the end.) The *faculty* of loving. A talent. A gift. 'We must always be a little in love,' Elizabeth Mayer said to me (at 70!) . . . Yes, but it becomes a difficult *task.* One that must be dissembled. Surrealism bores me. My gift depended on the flash—on the aperçu. The fake reason, the surface detail, language only—these give no joy. Jiménez kept on with the little flashes to the end. One can only remain open and wait."

A portrait of Bogan's good friend Elizabeth Mayer, written January 17, 1958, shows that Bogan had been preoccupied for a while with the gradual diminishment of her abilities. "Elizabeth Mayer: at age 75 she never for a moment either thinks she is old, or projects her age in mood or word. She is gradually thinning down, fading out, in her body; she shows no sign whatever of aging, in her mind or emotions. The books lie on the table; the piano is open and has music on it; she is going to the library tomorrow . . ." Near the end of her journal keeping, Bogan can do little more than maintain a log of the medication she takes and rail with bewilderment at the unhappiness that visits her each morning. Bogan's objective, direct rendering allows little room for self-pity but rather it describes how the inability to love or to find a source in which to place love drains off the will to live.

On June 22, 1959, she writes,

> Those nearest the heart drain off the first pity. How lovely they are, and how vulnerable! Their flesh, their very being draws out the misty love like a thread: over and over it wraps them round. Today they live; their names exquisitely clean and lies bright on their foreheads. They are young. Their bodies and their wishes will come to nothing. It is our purpose to wrap them round until they live inside a cocoon of this soft emotion which is part dread.
>
> They cannot see nor hear nor feel the love that pours out to them. Soft and delicate as fright in the dark, over and around them it goes. They sink into it. The heart pulls them down. "Forgive me; forgive me," the heart says, "You are beautiful and you will die. You are not really young, happy, or beautiful. You are appearance."

Although it is terrifying enough that her energy for work is fading, what terrifies her more is what lies behind the diminishment: a loss of faith or belief in anything. The first entry of the late journals describes the faith she had as a child in the meaning of things: "The difficulty was, in my childhood, that I expected everything to mean something. I believed in the pack of cards. I examined different packs with care, because the King, Queen, Jack were always different, under the unvarying signs of heart, club, diamond, and spade." Later, she recalls how "(within the rooms of houses, seen as a child from the outside) I thought that something must be going on: that people must be achieving something to assail the dreadful monotony of day after day. I trusted them to be doing something. Whatever it was, was as yet closed to me, but these fronts of building with afternoon light falling upon them with such terrible, dramatic effect—these certainly were important. Within them, life burned, a life in which I as yet had no part.

I believed this; from my soul I believed it." As if anticipating the approach of her own overwhelming doubt, eighteen months earlier she wrote, "What a pleasure and relief to have a faith or superstition of any kind! I should think that believers would dance with joy in the streets!"

If her waning artistic and physical powers made it difficult for her to hope and believe in a future, they were also leading her toward a confrontation with the person who was most responsible for having created Bogan's sense of hopelessness, her long-dead mother. She first recalls her mother in the hospital recovering from an unnamed operation. "The operation," she writes, "marked a kind of limit to my mother's *youthful* middle age, and brought in the worse hopes and lessened energies of a distinct later period." She remembers the hospital as being "private" and "yankee" and probably the result of a Dr. X who was one of her mother's lovers. The most important aspect of her memory however is the epiphany it produces for her when she recalls a vase of marigolds in her mother's hospital room. In contrast with a dozen pink roses sent to her by Dr. X, the marigolds, or "weeds," that passed for flowers from the uncultivated plots of her mill-town childhood, gave her "such a shock that I lost sight of the room for the moment . . . Suddenly I recognized something at once simple and full of the utmost richness of design and contrast that was mine. A whole world, in a moment, opened up: a world of design and simplicity; of a kind of rightness, a kind of taste and knowingness, that shot me forward, as it were, into an existence concerning which, up to that instant of recognition, I had had no knowledge or idea." Coupled then with the awareness of her own mother's diminishment is Bogan's awakening to a life of insight. The entry continues: "A garden from which such flowers came I could not visualize: I had never seen such a garden. But the impulse of pleasure that existed *back* of the arrangement (marigolds)—with its clear, rather severe emotional coloring—I knew."

It might be a stretch to say that this scene marks a moment of transference between Bogan and her mother, with the mother passing on, unconsciously, whatever physical power and spirit she possessed to her daughter. It is probably safer to claim that the late journals reveal, in scenes such as this, how Bogan was wrestling with the fact that like her mother, she too has passed over the threshold of vitality. Unlike the threshold she crossed over in the thirties when she tore herself down both as a poet and a person and reconstructed her art and life, the threshold crossed in the fifties leads to bleakness and despair. The late journals describe Bogan's constant struggle to reassure herself about the gains and achievements she has made not only as a poet but as a person who is capable of love.

In this process of reassurance Bogan finds a terrible likeness of herself in her mother: "Something which she thought ridiculous and unfinished in her face—as though part of her had stopped living or had not lived enough; and now, when resistance in the nerves or in the mind, or hope in the heart, was growing less, these unfinished things came out, in her face." And yet, at the same time she finds her own unfinished ambitions, her own emptiness mirrored in her mother's—in her memory of her mother—she finds, too, the flash, the aperçu, the occasion for a poem: "My mother had true elegance of hand. She could cut an apple like no one else. Her large hands guided the knife; the peel fell in a long light curve down from the fruit. Then she cut a slice from the side. The apple lay on the saucer, beautifully fresh, white, dewed with faint juice. She gave it to me. She put the knife away."

In another journal entry, this one from June 8, 1959, after ruminating about the process by which we remember our childhood, she is lead to a memory of her mother with the same suddenness from which the marigolds appeared. "People lived in intense worlds beyond me," she writes. "So that I do not at first see my mother. I see her clearly much later than I smell and feel her— long after I see those solid fractions of the houses and fields (these are of Ballardvale, etc.). She comes in frightfully clear, all at once." And this fright is associated with "the incredibly ugly mill towns of my childhood, barely dissociated from the empty, haphazardly cultivated, half wild, half deserted countryside around them." The flash or suddenness with which Bogan sees her mother, set against the familiar and ugly mill towns with their chaos, disorder, and dysfunction, is not entirely new to the journals. What is new, however, is the recognition that violence and trauma marked her early life. Later in the same entry, she writes, "I must have experienced violence from birth. But I remember it, at first, as only bound up with *flight*. I was bundled up and carried away." This passage serves as an introduction to a longer passage that details, with Breughel-like vividness, her memories of Milton, the mill town she lived in before Ballardvale, where "men and women bore ugly scars—of skin ailments, of boils, of carbuncles—on their faces, their necks, behind their ears" and where the "howl and whine of the wind rose at night." Bogan makes her deepest association with the violence and trauma of her early years, and with her mother, by noting how the mill flume was a primal source of fear: "The flume cascaded down the rocks, with bright sun sparkling on the clear foamy water. My mother was afraid of the flume. It had voices for her: it called and beckoned her. So I, too, began to fear it."

As if the mere recognition of having learned her fear of the flume from her mother is enough, Bogan ends her entry, but two days later, haunted by what she has remembered, she returns to finish recording the central and crucial scenes of childhood trauma. She writes: "But one (and final) scene of violence comes through. It is in lamplight, with strong shadows, and an open trunk is the center of it. The curved lid of the trunk is thrown back, and my mother is bending over the trunk, and packing things into it. She is crying and she screams. My father, somewhere in the shadows, groans as though he has been hurt. It is a scene of utmost terror. And then my mother sweeps me into her arms, and carries me out of the room. She is fleeing; she is running away." In the recollection of this scene, Bogan identifies a moment in which some of her own desires for freedom and love "had been early assassinated: shot dead." Bogan's prose is clear and objective and as such it carries no blame toward her mother nor does it ask for revenge or justice. In fact the writing shows great sympathy and understanding for her. "I never truly feared her," she concludes. "Her tenderness was the other side of her terror."

Although the image of the violent and dreadful mill towns, especially as they were represented in the old boarding and rooming houses, persisted throughout her life, it was the emotional and psychological violence inflicted on her by her parents, especially her mother, that she would be incapable of coming to terms with. The scene of flight, in which she realizes her desire for freedom and love had been "shot dead," is only a prelude to the most potent scene that Bogan records of her childhood.

The late journals represent a complex and even cautious activity. They begin on June 26, 1953, and end on July 28, 1966. During this thirteen-year interval, Bogan records twenty-eight entries. Twice she breaks from activity for almost four years. Several of the entries are long and rival in length and intensity of focus the three memoirs of the 1930s. Part of Bogan's cautiousness stems from her understanding of memory's effects. She writes on January 12, 1954: "The extraordinary thing about the revived experience [is] its power to bring back the moments in time, in place— the vignettes of pain, placed in a series of settings. Also the same sense of being trapped—of being used, of being made an *object*."

Although this entry is in response to her rereading of a series of letters Raymond Holden sent her during the summer of 1933, when Bogan traveled to Europe by herself on a Guggenheim Fellowship, as well as letters from Holden following the breakup of their marriage, the position it takes with regard to her past is consistent with what she comes to understand about the painful and traumatic scenes from her childhood. Both the early and late journals show that whenever Bogan begins to approach an incident from her past that is particularly difficult, she finds it necessary to write an extended qualification about the dangers of the "revived experience." In the aftermath of a particularly painful time in her childhood, she writes: "The secret family angers and secret disruptions passed over my head, it must have been for a year or so." And then without warning, "For two days, I went blind. I remember my sight coming back seeing that flat forked light of the gas flame, in its etched glass shade, suddenly appearing beside the bureau. What had I seen? I shall never know."

If events in her childhood had been so terrible that they resulted in blindness, she wondered how memory, with its opacities and occlusions, might penetrate to discover the truth. Bogan's dilemma was a complicated one and she wrestled with it courageously. In a June 8, 1959, entry she states: "One should set oneself the task, in full maturity, to fix on paper the bizarre, disordered, ungainly, furtive, mixed elements of one's life." But then a year later, September 17, 1960, she is less certain: "We must not bring back and describe 'the bad mother'—'the Dragon mother' in order to justify ourselves. Only to understand.—To hold the portrait of this evil figure unresolved, into age, into madness. It should be resolved in late youth." She ends this portion of the entry by referring to this unresolved evil figure as "the last Chinese box."

Throughout the late journals, Bogan is uncertain that she can reconcile herself to her mother, the tender yet terrible woman whose large, strong confident hands could peel an apple with elegance and eloquence and yet, in a moment, "could tear things to bits; put all their soft strength into thrusts and blows; they could lift objects so that they became threats of missiles." Finally, it is another memory of her mother's hands that opens the way for Bogan to get as close as she ever will to opening up the mystery of her mother. The memory is of the Ballardvale house, which she thought of as "the happiest in my life," a place of joy and order. The entry is from June 22, 1959: "In the hot afternoon she sat, by the parlor window, which was now striped with light. She put up the blind, and opened the shutters halfway, so that she could see and not be seen. She could look down over the sloping lawn to the sidewalk which ran beyond the maple tree and the fence. . . . She sat, shelling peas into a yellow bowl, or hulling strawberries. Sometimes I would sit in her lap, and smell the violet smell which was her own . . ."

In Milton, where Bogan lived before moving with her family to

Ballardvale, the mill dam flume represented the danger and darkness of the family's psyche, but in Ballardvale, in the relative order of their house on Oak Street, the danger lay in the small mill town itself and the trips her mother took to it. Continuing her entry of June 22, Bogan moves from her mother's "violet smell" to recalling that "when she dressed to go to town, the fear [Bogan's fear] came back. She could not dress without scattering things about the room. . . . She was careless about the order of a room, but carefully elegant about her own person." The activity surrounding her mother's dressing for town finds its focus for Bogan "in a bottle of Peau d'Espagne." "How I hated this perfume!" she exclaims. "It meant going to the city; it meant her other world; it meant trouble."

Trouble took a specific form as she and her brother became the object of their mother's anger. "Sometimes, when she was getting ready for church or for town, she would stand for long minutes, when she was already late, becoming more and more angry, the line of anger deepening between her eyes. . . . She was always late. She blamed everyone but herself for her lateness. We made her late. A dreadful chill came over our hearts."

The purposes for her mother's visits to town were not always clear and once she disappeared for "some weeks. No one knew where she had gone. Then suddenly she came back, thinner, as I remember, in totally different (shabby) clothes."

Out of the mixed and contradictory memories of Ballardvale, however, Bogan puts together a composite portrait of her mother that suffices as a partial antidote. She also comes to recognize some of her own character traits mirrored in her mother's. Again, this is from June 22: "A terrible, unhappy, lost, spoiled, bad-tempered child. A tender, contrite woman, with, somewhere in her blood, the rake's recklessness, the baffled artist's despair . . ."

The entries of June 1959 are as close as she comes to dealing with the darkest details of her childhood. The effort she puts into her journal at this time is the most concentrated and sustained in the period between 1953, when she returned to her journal, and 1966, when she died. These entries occupy the greatest number of pages, but unlike the coherent and burnished nature of the early journals and the memoirs, they signal a shift to a broken and fragmented syntax—a notational approach—that she uses until the end.

The June 1959 entries conclude with a recollection of her learning to read, and how the contents of her first reader, *Heart of Oak,* "were as delicious as food; they were food; they were the beginning of a new life. I had partially escaped. Nothing could really imprison me again. The door had opened, and I had begun to be free."

After setting this down, she does not return to her journal for more than year. When she does, on September 17, 1960, it is to warn herself away from bringing back the "bad mother." The entry about the "bad mother" ends with a short disquisition on the purpose of different disciplines and the role of the past: "The artist must resolve into art . . . the man of action into action . . . the philosopher into ideas. After a certain age one should glimpse it [the past] most often as a dream—or v. infrequently in *consciously* evoked meaning."

Curiously, the entry on September 17 ends with an unfinished paragraph about "the great kindling power of passionate love" in old age, and how age creates inhibition to such love especially in women. The fact that the unresolved portrait of the "evil mother" and unfulfilled feelings of passionate love appear in the same entry speaks directly to the complexity of emotions Bogan was trying to sort out as well as how much of her own passionate and sensual needs she identified with her mother.

The next day she copies out a passage from C. Day Lewis's "The Buried Day" and then quits her journal for another year, returning to it on September 7, 1961. Between September 7 and September 21, she makes five entries, all of them brief, telegraphic, and fragmentary. Reading these entries one detects a hesitancy and reluctance in Bogan to face the memories that are pushing forward, but the hesitancy results in a very slow movement toward what she in fact wants to avoid. On September 21, after a night of "Terrible dreams!" she describes the "lovely wind and rain" that arrives with the "tail-end of a hurricane." And she wonders, "Why do these storms come so far north? In the 19th century they kept to the southern tip of the continent." And then in an observation that can be understood as a metaphor for her own predicament, she says, "The earth has shifted infinitesimally on its axis."

What follows Bogan's comment about the weather and hurricane is the passage I quoted earlier in which she describes how the repressed material of the poet's life "becomes the poem." This attitude about the relationship between art and life appears in her journal, like an avoidance-approach technique, whenever she comes into the range of a particularly vivid detail from her past or a difficult memory. Instead of going on to meet the memory, she hides behind the insistence that "the poet represses the outright narrative of his life. He absorbs it, along with life itself. The repressed becomes the poem. Actually, I have written down my experience in the closest of detail. But the rough and vulgar facts are not there."

Inside of this aesthetic stance we can hear Bogan arguing with herself, saying on the one hand a poet must repress the outright narrative of his life while claiming on the other hand that she has written down her "experience in the closest of detail." What she fails to recognize but what a reader of her journals can see fairly easily is that the repressed details cannot stay repressed. They keep floating to the surface, buoyant with their own urgency.

Finally, near the end of the September 21, 1961, entry, Bogan seems to break this approach-avoidance pattern, although it happens almost inadvertently. After she puts down a short quotation by Chekhov, "'And all things are forgiven, and it would be strange not to forgive,'" she writes, "Forgiveness and the eagerness *to protect*—take care of, to endure. This Dr. Wall once said to me is the instinct of a little boy . . . Well, there it is I did manage to become a woman." Forgiveness, protection, endurance are the noble, self-sacrificing, as well as self-denying, attributes that Bogan has used to distance herself from the trauma of her childhood and to redeem it, as well as the "bad mother." Although Bogan has long been aware of these self-preserving mechanisms, confronting them now, perhaps at a point in her life when she feels there is nothing left to lose, she can admit, "Now, in my later years, I have no hatred or resentment left. But I still cannot describe some of the nightmares lived through, with love. So I shan't describe them at all. Finished. Over." But not quite over, because now she writes the most shocking and indelible memory of her mother: "The door is open, and I see the ringed hand on the pillow; I weep by the hotel window as she goes down the street, with *another;* I stare at the dots which make up the newspaper photograph (which makes me realize I had not yet learned to read.) The chambermaid tells me to stop crying. How do we survive such things? But it is long over. And forgiven . . ."

Yes, forgiven, but not forgotten, not ever to be forgotten, although constantly repressed.

After she records what she has only moments before said she "shan't describe," Bogan eloquently provides a corrective to the crude shock of having witnessed her mother's adultery at an age when Bogan had not yet begun to read. The fact that she couldn't read is significant given that Bogan marks her first emancipation from the depravations of her childhood with the advent of her literacy. Witnessing her mother's adultery came at a time when she had not yet acquired the means to escape from her surroundings through books and language and as such the image of her mother's hand on the pillow, the wedding ring drawing her attention, lay deeply repressed but smoldering with lifelong intensity. As if to make up for setting down that which she pledged not to, Bogan writes, "The regions and countries of the dream. The unconscious makes its repeated mistakes; it has not *seen* the reality; it has sensed it merely . . . A reflection; a distortion . . . And it repeats its mistakes, as though it had learned them by rote."

As she comes to the conclusion of the September 21 entry she muses about love and another familiar theme, the lateness of the hour in her life. But this is only a pause before she pushes on to her final understanding, her final antidote: "How can we explain the places where we finally land, after the inexplicable journeys, long boring holidays, years of misapprehension? How do we finally find them—or do they find us, like a happening coming after a dream which follows the dream's speech and action, so that we say it is our 'dream out' . . ."

When she finishes the September 21 entry, she will stay away from her journal for another four years, and when she comes back to it she is in the grip of a depression equal to the one that held her thirty years earlier.

Reading Bogan's journals it is sometimes easy to forget that especially from 1953 to 1964, she is active as a reviewer, teacher, lecturer, letter writer, and poet. The struggle the journals reflect is one that takes place almost entirely within her. From 1964 until the time of her death, however, her depression debilitates and imprisons her almost completely, and although she struggles to keep up her literary activities and fights to remain open to the muse's visits, the extreme isolating effect of her depression makes it difficult for her to stay engaged. In fact, a very strong impression we derive from the last journal entries is that although Bogan has not literally landed in one of the fearful boardinghouses of her childhood, she is a prisoner of the mentality of those places. Witnessing the disintegration of Bogan's physical and emotional state, it is difficult to remember the determined woman who sought in her journal of the early 1950s a way to "the capable and free setting down of 'memory and desire' . . . of what I have become, and what I know." Thirteen years later, it is nearly inconceivable that she could write: "The feel of the pen moving across the paper should be curative. That and *some* attempt to listen to music.—Who have I become? What has me in hand?"

Borges and His Precursors

IN GRADUATE SCHOOL when I began to read Latin American poets such as César Vallejo and Pablo Neruda in a serious way, I was still no more than a superficial reader of Walt Whitman. Nevertheless, I could see how important the work of Whitman was to these poets who wrote about the common man and the twentieth-century social and political forces that ruled their lives. Once I began to engage Whitman more fully, it became clear that Vallejo and Neruda, as well as other Latin American poets, had come to a quicker and more resolute understanding of Whitman than had my countrymen. Although Allen Ginsberg and the second-generation Beats had done much to bring Whitman alive, especially for my generation, the general perception concerning North America's self-proclaimed American bard was still closer to Donald Hall's description of Whitman as the sort of embarrassing uncle or second cousin who shows up at a family wedding or funeral wearing a wide necktie with a palm tree painted on it.

Borges in *An Introduction to American Literature* reminds us that "all the so-called civic poetry, or poetry of involvement, of our times is descended from Walt Whitman" and that this influence "is prolonged in Sandburg and Neruda." Few United States poets of the last half of the twentieth century and perhaps fewer now are much enamored of Sandburg, but Neruda? Yes, Neruda has become a kind of exotic staple for us and many of us have enough Spanish from high school or college to be able to read the words on the page, even if we don't always know what they mean.

Near the end of graduate school I sketched out an essay that tried to describe the circuitous route that Whiman's influence followed. I wanted to prove that Whitman became a more potent influence on U.S. poets for having been imported back to the states by way of Latin America. When I was struck by this idea almost thirty years ago, it seemed ironic, mysterious, and even profound to me. In my essay I did not dwell long on the repatriation of Whitman. I thought it was the exception to rules of influence which I imagined described lineal successions, causes and effects: Wyatt goes to the Continent, brings back the sonnet, which gets passed to Surrey, Spenser, Sidney, and Shakespeare, etc. Or more dramatically, a messenger from God appears in a dream to Caedmon and demands of the tone-deaf shepherd, "Sing me a song!" And suddenly and divinely Caedmon becomes the first English poet. Although I had read T. S. Eliot's essay "Tradition and the Individual Talent" and was familiar with his belief that the existing order of literature is changed by the arrival of something new and as such "the past [is] altered by the present as much as the present is directed by the past," I was not astute enough to apply it to this particular instance. I was still too much a student of poetry and not a student of the dream that poetry creates to be able to see that poetry invites a reader into a world that demolishes linear and lineal programs of history.

At the time I attempted my essay, I had already encountered Borges's essay "Kafka and His Precursors," for one of the books that was assigned frequently in college literature courses of the late 1960s and early 1970s and which was almost as ubiquitous as Ferlinghetti's *A Coney Island of the Mind* was the New Directions *Labyrinths,* a copy of which I acquired very early on in my rampage of literature. When I first read "Kafka and His Precursors," I was not equipped intellectually to recognize the radical reformation it contains concerning literary influence or precursors. In this essay, Borges discusses a group of stories that predate Kafka. Each of these stories is concerned with paradox. By slightly shifting his point of view and by reading the stories through an irony-tinted lens, Borges is able to show how Kafka's work changes our perception and understanding of the precursor stories. Toward the end of Borges's essay, we find this clear formulation of what he is after: "The poem 'Fears and Scruples' by Browning foretells Kafka's work, but our reading of Kafka perceptively sharpens and deflects our reading of the poem. Browning did not read it [his poem] as we do now." One feels that this insight, which is elegantly and efficiently put before us, is something we have always known but could not realize until Borges formulated it.

Because Borges is such a thorough and self-scrutinizing writer and thinker the momentum of his idea does not stop with a consideration of Kafka. Borges has outlined a general principle that allows him to leap past its formulation concerning one author, to a startling and provocative conclusion: "The fact is that every writer creates his own precursors. His work modifies our conception of the past, as it will modify the future. In this correlation the identity or plurality of the men involved is unimportant."

The plurality or identity of the men involved is probably not important to a metaphysical or ideal notion of poetry, though it is important for providing an entrance, via the wormhole of personality, into the world of any aesthetic construct. What Borges wants to show is that a writer or poet is alive in proportion to the number of precursors he or she is able to create and in this manifold community his or her identity is subsumed but not lost. Whitman wrote in "Starting from Paumanok," "I conn'd old times, / I sat studying at the feet of the great masters, / Now if eligible O that the great masters might return and study me."

Using Borges's essay "Kafka and His Precursors" as a guide, I'll explore Borges's influence not on a current or even a future writer but on an American writer of the past, Ralph Waldo Emerson. By taking up Borges and Emerson in this fashion, I hope to show how Emerson, the American Plato, is sharpened and deflected by the younger Borges and how, to use Whitman's conceit, the great master of transcendentalism returns to study at the feet of his own acolyte.

Although Borges makes a case for the insignificance of "identity or plurality" of authorship, he would have agreed with Emerson's seemingly simpler notion of "elective affinities" where "like draws to like." Borges was drawn to Emerson, as he has written, because he was an "intellectual poet who has ideas": "he had ideas and was thoroughly a poet." In Borges's "The Other Death," a character states that Emerson is "a poet far more complex, far more skilled, and truly more extraordinary than the unfortunate Poe." Like Emerson, Borges was an intellectual poet—a poet of ideas—who was also thoroughly a poet of the heart and soul. Not everyone holds this opinion about Borges. James Woodall, one of his biographers, excluded from his account any discussion of Borges's poems because he agreed with another Borges scholar, John Sturrock, that the poems are "thoughtful, tight-lipped, and perhaps a little dull." Both Emerson and Borges did not have purely intellectual notions about the function and purpose of poetry and the poet, however. Regardless of the remarkable force of their intellects they never lost sight of the fact that poems begin in "emotion." Borges once remarked that poetry should not be "attempted without emotion. It is in that case a mere game of words. . . . When I write, I always begin by emotion," he said. "And then I go to words. I don't begin by words. . . . words are given me after the emotion, after that exhilaration."

Borges's and Emerson's lives share many similarities. Both men were very popular speakers; their livelihoods, especially in Emerson's case, depended on the lectures and talks they delivered to a wide range of groups. They were raised by women. Both were avid readers, though they were not programmatic. They followed their interests and instincts. Borges complained about the concept of compulsory reading; he said there should only be "compulsory happiness." Perhaps most importantly they were both born at the beginning of centuries, Emerson in 1803 and Borges in 1899, and as a result they were able to take advantage of revolutionary cultural movements, romanticism and modernism, respectively, without having to be revolutionaries themselves. Borges and Emerson embody T. S. Eliot's affirmation in "The Music of Poetry" that in art there are innovators and developers, as Eliot himself was a developer of symbolist notions. Both Borges and Emerson were also very interested in classification not as an end in itself but as a way of resisting the notion of historical progress and as a way of representing ideal relationships. We can see the result of this in Borges's labyrinth and Emerson's conception of nature.

Additionally, Borges felt enormous sympathy for Emerson's eclectic interests and what in *An Introduction to North American Literature* he calls the multiple roots of transcendentalism, which touched "Hindu pantheism, Neoplatonic speculations, the Persian mystics, the visionary theology of Swedenborg, German idealism, and the writings of Coleridge and Carlyle."

Regarding influence and one's precursors, Borges and Emerson shared similar ideas about the obligation writers have to the past. When he addressed students at Columbia University in the 1970s Borges suggested that an apprentice writer "should begin, of course, by imitating the writers he likes. This is the way the writer becomes himself through losing himself—that strange way of double living, of living in reality as much as one can and at the same time of living in that other reality, the one he has to create, the reality of dreams" (*Borges on Writing,* di Giovanni, 164). Emerson, commenting in his essay "Experience," remarked that "dream delivers us to dream, and there is no end to illusion." He also believed that identifying with writers from the past was the way to finding one's self as a writer. Quoting Goethe, one of his heroes, Emerson liked to say, "The greatest genius will never be worth much if he pretends to draw exclusively from his own resources." And, Goethe again, "What is genius but the faculty of seizing on and turning to account any thing that strikes us . . . every one of my writings has been furnished to me by a thousand different persons, a thousand different things." Borges called those who furnished his own genius with resources for his work, "benefactors," bestowing upon them a courtly function, and seeing himself as the recipient of their benefices. What Emerson and Borges recognize is the negligible role originality plays in one's art. Or perhaps I should say that art is original as it relates to origins and beginnings rather than spontaneous eruptions or undigested expressiveness. T. S. Eliot reminds us of this in his sly formulation, which has been widely paraphrased: "Good poets borrow and great poets steal."

As I noted earlier both Borges and Emerson were voracious readers. After Borges's blindness engulfed him he reread books by remembering them. He had a dedicated group of people who read to him and was in the habit of correcting them when they made a mistake or left out a passage. Emerson, it seems, had invented a method of speed-reading that sent him scrabbling over a page like a goat over a rocky landscape. In his essay "The Poet," Emerson writes, "An imaginative book renders us much more service at first by stimulating us through its tropes, than afterward when we arrive at the precise sense of the author. I think nothing is of any value in books excepting the transcendental and extraordinary." And as if he had Borges's compulsory happiness in mind, he continues, "How cheap even the liberty [produced by reading] then seems; how mean to study, when an emotion communicates to the intellect the power to sap and upheave nature; how great the perspective! Nations, times, systems, enter and disappear like threads in a tapestry of a large figure and many colors; dream delivers us to dream, and while the drunkenness lasts we will sell our bed, our philosophy, our religion, in our opulence."

Their debt to writers of the past was so deep because their reading, their compulsion to seek out this opulent happiness, allowed them to live so thoroughly in the dream of life. It is Borges who remarks in his story "The Zahir" that "idealist doctrine has it that the verbs 'to live' and 'to dream' are at every point synonymous; for me, thousands upon thousands of appearances will pass into one; a complex dream will pass into a simple one. Others will dream that I am mad, while I dream of the Zahir. When every man on earth thinks, day and night, of the Zahir, which will be dream and which reality, the earth or the Zahir?" Likewise, Emerson knew well this synonymous experience. While reading Montaigne, he found, "It seemed as if I had written the book myself in some former life" (Richardson, 69).

In "The Flower of Coleridge," Borges expresses not only the precept of idealist doctrine concerning the verbs *to live* and *to dream,* but he demonstrates the validity of what Emerson experienced while reading Montaigne. In fact, at the start of the piece, he quotes a passage from Emerson's essay "The Nominalist and the Realist": "I am very much struck in literature by the appearance that one person wrote all the books; . . . there is such equality and identity both of judgment and point of view in the narrative that it is plainly the work of one all-seeing, all-hearing gentleman." By treating Emerson's perception as if it were real and not merely a speculation, Borges confirms Emerson's claim, which itself is built on Shelley's remark: "that all the poems of the past, present, and future were episodes or fragments of a single infinite poem, written by all the poets of the earth." Borges's method for creating this reality is to recite in etymological fashion, the history of an object, a person, event, or idea. This method, which he uses frequently, is found in one of its purest manifestations at the beginning of "The Zahir."

In Buenos Aires the Zahir is a common twenty-centavo coin into which a razor or letter opener has scratched the letters N T and the number 2; the date stamped on the face is 1929. (In Gujarat, at the end of the eighteenth century, the Zahir was a tiger; in Java it was a blind man in the Surakarta mosque, stoned by the faithful; in Persia, an astrolabe that Nadir Shah ordered thrown into the sea; in the prisons of Mahdi, in 1892, a small sailor's compass, wrapped in a shred of cloth from a turban, that Rudolf Karl von Slatin touched; in the synagogue in Córdoba, according to Zotenberg, a vein in the marble of one of the twelve hundred pillars; in the ghetto in Tetuan, the bottom of a well.)

As one critic has noted, Borges's "approach to poetic language might have had an archaeological cast" (*Borges, the Poet,* 103). Close readers of Borges don't need to be so tentative about this claim. Borges was fond of promoting Emerson's notion that "all words are metaphors—or fossil poetry." In Borges's excavations of a word or image, however, we don't only discover the intertextual relationships between authors nor merely the proof of the living dream; Borges's excavations give us access to the origins of literary artifacts and tropes. His etymological lists are as much as anything epic catalogs, that procrustean device Homer, or someone, must have used to both help him remember how to tell the story of the Trojan War and to create an image equal to his task. For what is an epic catalog but the stylus of Adam's naming stuck in one groove of the world? From this as well we begin to understand the universal nature of any epic undertaking and how it recreates itself through the centuries and millennia as an image of the imagination's attempt to fashion a universal history.

Universal history, as Borges has it, contains the germ of Emerson's notion that "the use of natural history is to give aid in supernatural history; the use of the outer creation to give us language for the beings and changes of inward creation." Borges follows "natural history" as it transforms into universal history through the imagination's ability to detect multiplicity and simultaneity, the kind we have seen in "The Zahir" and in Emerson's "all-seeing and all-hearing gentleman." Whereas Emerson believed multiplicity leads to a spiritual and transcendental ideal, and ultimately becomes a source of consoling truth, Borges believed it led to a more ironic and paradoxical understanding, an existential confrontation with the human predicament. There is very little in Borges that is meant to console but there is, nevertheless, much that transcends the entropy of the disconsolate. His truth is the sublime beauty of paradox. "A man sets out to draw the world. As the years go by," Borges writes, again in "The Zahir," "he peoples a space with images of provinces, kingdoms, mountains, bays, ships, islands, fishes, rooms, instruments, stars, horses, and individuals. A short time before he dies, he discovers that that patient labyrinth of lines traces the lineaments of his own face." In "The Zahir," he says of Teodelina Villar lying in her coffin: "No version of that face that had so disturbed me shall ever be as memorable as this one; really, since it could almost be the first, it ought to be the last" (243).

Although Emerson understood the repetitive nature of existence, and he would readily agree with Borges that "there is no coin that is not the symbol of all the coins that shine endlessly down throughout history and fable" ("The Zahir," 244) or "that there is nothing however humble that does not imply the history of the world and its infinite concatenation of cause and effects," he could not embrace, given his Unitarianism, the profound indifference of the universe, as Borges did. Yet Emerson came close to it. In his essay "Experience," he admits, "I am a fragment and this [essay] is a fragment of me." And further, "Life has no memory. That which proceeds in succession might be remembered, but that which is coexistent, or ejaculated from a deeper cause, as yet far from being conscious, knows not its own tendency." We can understand Emerson better for the deflection Borges's twentieth-century alienation and isolation brings to him as one of his precursors. Just as Kafka's Castle makes manifest Zeno's paradox or supports the parables of Kierkegaard, Borges's essays and poems help us to excavate Emerson beyond the hopeful salvation and redemption the transcendentalist could not keep himself from dreaming. Emerson's essay "Circles" perhaps gives us the best perspective on this relationship as well as strong evidence the American Plato knew well the interior of Borges's labyrinth. "Circles" begins not with the description of a circle but of a sphere: "Nature centres into balls / And her proud ephemerals, / Fast to surface and outside, / Scan the profile of the sphere; / Knew they what that signified, / A new genesis were here." A sphere, as opposed to a circle, has dimension, though both figures have centers that are equidistant to their parts. Emerson says his circle/sphere is "the highest emblem in the cipher of the world." In order to illustrate his point, he tells us "St. Augustine described the nature of God as a circle whose centre was everywhere and its circumference nowhere." Emerson's preoccupation with this cipher is merely another chapter, another example, of what Borges called "universal history."

In "The Fearful Sphere of Pascal," Borges writes, "Perhaps universal history is the history of a few metaphors." The history Borges constructs from the sphere, of course, is not one based on progress and development but on preservation and reiteration. His catalog of thinkers who employ the sphere in their dream of the world includes Plato, Xenophanes, Parmenides of Elea, the Sicilian Empedocles, Dante, Rabelais, Giordano Bruno, right down to Pascal, and now we can include Emerson. The differences between these thinkers, Borges tells us is "intonation." Intonation is what precursors provide to the future. Intonation is the subtlest characteristic of the prophetic. Pascal found his sphere frightful or terrible. "The absolute space that had been a liberation for Bruno," Borges says, "was a labyrinth and an abyss for Pascal." Emerson's intonations concerning the circle are subtler than Pascal's. On the surface, so to speak, they sound hopeful: "The life of man is a self-evolving circle, which, from a ring imperceptibly small, rushes on all sides outward to new and larger circles, and that without end." But the pentimento beneath this optimistic concentricism reveals an intonation of something darker, less certain, more, yes, Borgesian, as the following passages, taken from Emerson, demonstrate. "Our life is an apprenticeship to the truth that around every circle another can be drawn; that there is no end in nature but every end is a beginning; that there is always another dawn risen on mid-noon, and under every deep a lower deep opens." "There are no fixtures in nature." "Everything looks permanent until its secret is known." "Every man is not so much a workman in the world as he is a suggestion of what he should be." "In my daily work I incline to repeat my old steps and do not believe in remedial force, in the power of change and reform." And finally, "The one thing we seek with insatiable desire is to forget ourselves, to be surprised out of propriety, to lose our sempiternal memory and to do something without knowing how or why."

Without Borges, Emerson's intonation would remain transcendental, mystical, and pantheistic as if it were the sound of a diffuse light emanating from the center of *his* labyrinth. But Borges's work forces us to see that the transcendental—the labyrinth—is a form of the abyss from which no light emanates, and as such it alters forever the way we read his great precursor.

REFERENCES

Borges, Jorge Luis. "The Zahir," in *Labyrinths: Selected Stories and Other Writings*. New York: New Directions, 1964.

Cortinez, Carlos, ed. *Borges, the Poet*. Fayetteville: University of Arkansas Press, 1986.

di Giovanni, Norman Thomas, Daniel Halpern, and Frank McShane, eds. *Borges on Writing*. New York: Dutton, 1973.

Richardson, Jr., Robert D. *The Mind on Fire*. Berkeley: University of California Press, 1995.

Woodall, James. *Borges: A Life*. New York: Basic Books, 1996.

II

A Familiar Gratuity

⟨∞⟩

AT THE END OF THE MONTHS Hart Crane spent on Isle of Pines, Cuba, May–October 1926, a hurricane passed over the island and all but destroyed Villa Casas, the disheveled plantation his maternal grandfather had built. One of the reasons Crane had gone to the Caribbean was to undertake repairs on the house and grounds that his grandmother and mother had long neglected. The storm more or less settled the fate of the family estate as well as put an end to the most productive period of writing Crane would ever experience. During his time on the island he made substantial progress on *The Bridge* and he started a number of descriptive lyrics, "Island Quarry," "The Air Plant," "O Carib Isle!," "The Air Plant," and "Royal Palm," as well as "Eternity." Compared to the visionary expansiveness of *The Bridge,* these are poems written in a minor key—touristic, direct, and accessible. They also lack the ambitious self-consciousness of Crane's longer masterpieces. Paul Mariani in his biography of Crane reports that the poet thought of these poems as "anthology pieces" and described them to Yvor Winters as "considerably clipped." Crane's affection for these poems was muted because his aspiration for Parnassian fame lay with the unfinished epic, *The Bridge.*

Nevertheless this group of *plein air* poems, written directly from his experiences on Isle of Pines and his visits to Havana and Grand Cayman, are some of the most finished and powerful poems Crane produced. "Eternity" is the least finished of these, though it is the most direct and most faithful and consistent in its use of colloquial diction. In it Crane looks past his near contemporary Marianne Moore and ahead to the prosaic artfulness of Elizabeth Bishop. Especially when compared with Crane's "The Hurricane," which begins "Lo, Lord, Thou ridest! / Lord, Lord, Thy swifting heart // Nought stayeth, nought now bideth / But's smithereened apart!," "Eternity" feels spontaneous, talky, unstudied. We know that "The Hurricane" was written before Crane had experienced a serious tropical storm. It is less about an external climatic event than it is about an internal, spiritual typhoon. It is about the interior chaos that was Crane's habitual condition and in this way it partakes in the metaphysical tumble and boil of so much of Crane's work. As such it is something of modernism's own antidote to the objective correlative.

"Eternity" and the other descriptive lyrics he wrote about the Caribbean as well as a few early poems such as "My Grandmother's Love Letters," "Repose of Rivers," and "Passage," among others are, to my mind, more satisfying and convincing, if less provocative. It may be that I am drawn to them because of the dramatic contrast they create with the rest of Crane's work but I'm certain, too, that I admire them because of the way Williams and his particular strain of American idiom bleeds through. At such an intersection I find the visionary wrestling with the merchant, straw and mud tramped into the vestibule of the church. In other words I hear the human voice that can't help itself from speaking as a poet rather than the poet who tries to speak like a god or angel.

In its own way "Eternity" is quite lavish. Its exaggerations, "Parts of the roof reached Yucatan, I suppose," serve as comic relief, a buffer from the horrific destruction that was nearly fatal to Crane. The effect of the reportorial style of "Eternity" creates a strange and confounding world out of the destroyed literal world: "But was there a boat? By the wharf's old site you saw / Two decks unsandwiched, split sixty feet apart / And a funnel high and dry up near the park / Where a frantic peacock rummaged amid a heap of cans." Tragedy is inherent in such a scene, as is melodrama, but Crane avoids the latter, giving us instead a rueful, dark humor: "Back at the erstwhile house / We shoveled and sweated; watched the ogre sun / blister the mountain, stripped now, bare of palm / Everything—and lick the grass, as black as patent / Leather, which the rimed white wind had glazed."

I particularly like "Eternity" for the clarity of its postapocalyptic "vision." "Eternity" anticipates the genre of nuclear and human holocaust poems that is one of the twentieth century's difficult legacies, and those horses of the apocalypse that appear in Edwin Muir's "The Horses" and Philip Levine's "Horse," or in Basil Bunting's "Chomei at Toyama," which among other events recounts the destruction by earthquake of twelfth-century Kyoto. Perhaps the strangest moment in "Eternity" is when the horses appear in their "strange gratuity." "Gratuity" is a word that Crane had employed in other poems and is meant to indicate the inexplicable and mysterious nature of experience. The brilliance of this passage is that Crane manages to authenticate by means of "Don," the identifiable horse, the assessable and literal destructive effects of the storm, while the other horse, the "white" one, authenticates the lasting and unknown effects of the storm; it is a "phantom maned by all that memoried night of screaming rain— Eternity!" This is about as much lyric uplift as the otherwise plainspoken poem can handle without becoming melodramatic. Or maybe it *is* slightly melodramatic but we are forgiving of its excess. Regardless, the magnitude of excess in "Eternity" is considerably less than the excess of the unironic poeticisms of "The Hurricane," its weird counterpart.

Although some might feel "Eternity" resolves itself too easily ("The fever was checked"), I like the way the quotidian returns to shore up the world. After all, Crane has been telling a story: "I stood a long time in Mack's talking / New York with the gobs, Guantanamo, Norfolk—, / Drinking Bacardi and talking U.S.A.," and the point of the story for him was his precarious survival, which he had learned to celebrate over the years with drink and sailors—his familiar gratuity.

ETERNITY

September—remember!
October—all over.
—BARBADIAN ADAGE

After it was over, though still gusting balefully,
The old woman and I foraged some drier clothes
And left the house, or what was left of it;
Parts of the roof reached Yucatan, I suppose.
She almost—even then—got blown across lots
At the base of the mountain. But the town, the town!

Wires in the streets and Chinamen up and down
With arms in slings, plaster strewn dense with tiles,
And Cuban doctors, troopers, trucks, loose hens . . .
The only building not sagging on its knees,
Fernandez' Hotel, was requisitioned into pens
For cotted Negroes, bandaged to be taken
To Havana on the first boat through. They groaned.

But was there a boat? By the wharf's old site you saw
Two decks unsandwiched, split sixty feet apart
And a funnel high and dry up near the park
Where a frantic peacock rummaged amid heaped cans.
No one seemed to be able to get a spark
From the world outside, but some rumor blew
That Havana, not to mention poor Batabanó,
Was halfway under water with fires
For some hours since—all wireless down
Of course, there too.

                Back at the erstwhile house
We shoveled and sweated; watched the ogre sun
Blister the mountain, stripped now, bare of palm,
Everything—and lick the grass as black as patent
Leather, which the rimed white wind had glazed.
Everything gone—or strewn in riddled grace—
Long tropic roots high in the air, like lace.
And somebody's mule steamed, swaying right by the pump,
Good God! as though his sinking carcass there

Were death predestined! You held your nose already
Along the roads, begging for buzzards, vultures . . .
The mule stumbled, staggered. I somehow couldn't budge
To lift a stick for pity of his stupor.

For I

Remember still that strange gratuity of horses
—One ours, and one a stranger, creeping up with dawn
Out of the bamboo brake through howling sheeted light
When the storm was dying. And Sarah saw them, too—
Sobbed. Yes, now—it's almost over. For they know;
The weather's in their noses. There's Don—but that one, white
—I can't account for him! And true, he stood
Like a vast phantom maned by all that memoried night
Of screaming rain—Eternity!

Yet water, water!

I beat the dazed mule toward the road. He got that far
And fell dead or dying, but it didn't so much matter.

The morrow's dawn was dense with carrion hazes
Sliding everywhere. Bodies were rushed into graves
Without ceremony, while hammers pattered in town.
The roads were being cleared, injured brought in
And treated, it seemed. In due time
The President sent down a battleship that baked
Something like two thousand loaves on the way.
Doctors shot ahead from the deck of planes.
The fever was checked. I stood a long time in Mack's talking
New York with the gobs, Guantanamo, Norfolk,—
Drinking Bacardi and talking U.S.A.

Hart Crane (1927)

On Whitman's
"To a Locomotive in Winter"

⬧

IN WORDSWORTH'S 1833 SONNET, "Steamboats, Viaducts, and Railways," the poet of recollection and tranquility is forced to look into the future by these conveyances and conveyors, these "Motions and Means," to consider how they might "mar / The loveliness of Nature" and "prove a bar / To the Mind's gaining that prophetic sense / Of future change . . . whence / May be discovered what in soul ye are." Regardless of how "harsh" these features are, Wordsworth concedes that they should be embraced by "Nature" because they are products of "Man's art."

> Motions and Means, on land and sea at war
> With old poetic feeling, not for this,
> Shall ye, by Poets even, be judged amiss!
> Nor shall your presence, howsoe'er it mar
> The loveliness of Nature, prove a bar
> To the Mind's gaining that prophetic sense
> Of future change, that point of vision, whence
> May be discovered what in soul ye are.
> In spite of all that beauty may disown
> In your harsh features, Nature doth embrace
> Her lawful offspring in Man's art; and Time,
> Pleased with your triumphs o'er his brother Space,
> Accepts from your bold hands the proffered crown
> Of hope, and smiles on you with cheer sublime.

Although it is interesting to see how willingly Wordsworth makes art of metal and steel—the interchangeable part rushing to meet the assembly line—what is as equally interesting to me is the way the diction of the title stands in stark contrast to the diction of the poem itself. Steamboat, viaduct, and railway are all words that came into use during Wordsworth's lifetime. This crowding in of the thingness and man-made particularity of the contemporary world is rare in Romantic poets, who were apt to subscribe to John Baillie's notion of the sublime in which "Vast objects occasion vast Sensations." Nevertheless, in Wordsworth, more than in Keats, Shelley, Coleridge, and Byron, we can see it beginning to encroach, for example in Book VII of the *Prelude,* "London Residency" and, in another sonnet, "Composed upon Westminster Bridge, September 3, 1802." Wordsworth's recognition of these things is grudging and one feels his conviction is powered more by an argument that attempts to extend the range of the sublime—an aesthetic notion—rather than by a deeply held belief.

Almost exactly a century later, Hart Crane can talk rather easily about the "Machine Age," but like Wordsworth, he still needs to make a case for the worthiness of the machine as a poetic emblem. In his brief 1930 essay, "Modern Poetry," he writes, "For unless poetry can absorb the machine, i.e., *acclimatize* it as naturally and casually as trees, cattle, galleons, castles and all other human associations of the past, then poetry has failed of its full contemporary function." I don't mean to suggest that no progress was made between 1833 and 1930. In fact Crane is arguing that machines must lose their "glamour" so that they appear in their "true subsidiary order in human life as use and continual poetic allusion subdue [their] novelty." Both Wordsworth and Crane share notions about how language becomes imbued or endowed with human associations and how experience is "converted," in Crane's words, by the "spontaneity and gusto" of the poet. Wordsworth, for his part in "Steamboats, Viaducts, and Railways," describes "the Mind's gaining that prophetic sense / Of future change, that point of vision."

At the end of Crane's essay, which was included in Oliver M. Sayler's *Revolt in the Arts: A Survey of the Creation, Distribution and Appreciation of Art in America,* he makes this statement: "The most typical and valid expression of the American *psychosis* seems to me still to be found in Whitman." By "psychosis" he means generally unstable conditions out of which art is made in America and the uncertain mixing of "influential traditions of English prosody which form points of departure, at least, for any indigenous rhythms and forms which may emerge." In Whitman, Crane found someone who "was able to coordinate those forces in America which seem most intractable, fusing them into a universal vision which takes on added significance as time goes on."

While Wordsworth and Crane express differing levels of anxiety about the relationship of poetry to the materiality of the industrial and modern eras, Whitman expresses none. "I will make the poems from materials," he writes in "Starting from Paumanok," "for I think they are to be the most spiritual poems." Instead of reserving the sublime for Baillie's "vast objects," Whitman argues for a sublime of "objects gross" that are "one" with "the unseen soul" ("A Song for Occupations"). In Wordsworth it is rare to come upon steamships, viaducts, and railways. And in Crane we find them used strategically. But in Whitman they are common and ordinary. He catalogs things, places, occupations, tools, machines, and all manner of modern objects the way Homer lists ships and warriors or the Old Testament tribes. From "Song of Myself" to "Song of the Broad Axe" and "Song for Occupations," Whitman "peruse[s] manifold objects" and finds that no two are "alike, and everyone good, / The earth good and the stars good, and their adjuncts all good" ("Song of Myself").

In his headlong, magpie manner, Whitman rarely lingers on these "adjuncts," he merely piles them up like cordwood, which is in keeping with the inclusive method of his epic. Size and value are plentiful, while finesse and analysis are at a premium. Nevertheless, Whitman does occasionally stop his listing and cataloging obsessions and stares hard at an object, the way he does in "To a Locomotive in Winter," published in 1879.

Thee for my recitative,
Thee in the driving storm even as now, the snow, the winter-day
    declining,
Thee in thy panoply, thy measur'd dual throbbing and thy beat
    convulsive,
Thy black cylindric body, golden brass, and silvery steel,
Thy ponderous side-bars, parallel and connecting rods, gyrating,
    shuttling at thy sides,
Thy metrical, now swelling pant and roar, now tapering in the
    distance,
Thy great protruding head-light fix'd in front,
Thy long, pale, floating vapor-pennants, tinged with delicate
    purple,
The dense and murky clouds out-belching from thy smoke-stack,
Thy knitted frame, thy springs and valves, the tremulous twinkle
    of thy wheels
Thy train of cars behind, obedient, merrily-following,
Through gale or calm, now swift, now slack, yet steadily
    careering;
Type of the modern—emblem of motion and power—pulse of
    the continent,
For once come serve the Muse and merge in verse, even as here I
    see thee,
With storm and buffeting gusts of wind, and falling snow,
By day thy warning ringing bell to sound its notes,
By night thy silent signal lamps to swing.

Fierce-throated beauty!
Roll through my chant with all thy lawless music, thy swinging
    lamps at night,
Thy madly-whistled laughter, echoing, rumbling like an
    earthquake, rousing all,
Law of thyself complete, thine own track firmly holding,
(No sweetness debonair of tearful harp or glib piano thine,)
Thy trills of shrieks by rocks and hills return'd,
Launch'd o'er the prairies wide, across the lakes,
To the free skies unpent and glad and strong.

What Whitman has created in this poem is a kind of template that could serve for writing odes about any number of things and objects found in his lists and catalogs, i.e., a "steam printing press," a "calking-iron," a "cutter's cleaver," a "snow-sleigh," an "electric telegraph," or a "thrashing-machine," etc., etc. These, like locomotives, are "type[s] of the modern" and "emblems of motion and power—pulse of the continent." The emblematic nature of these objects demands that we regard them in the present. In order to emphasize this Whitman declares, "Even now," in the second line of "To a Locomotive in Winter," and later, "here I see thee." The modern moment is present and urgent and the objects that occupy it contain its "motion and power." It is not something conjured in a spot of time and it is not something remembered or reflected upon in tranquility. It whistles "madly," it rumbles "like an earthquake," and it swells and "pant[s]," and "roar[s]" erotically. How different and unequivocal is this compared with Thoreau's ambivalence for the Fitchburg Railroad that passed near Walden Pond.

One of the great contributions Whitman made to American poetry was the way in which he enlarged the range of its diction and almost single-handedly created a reservoir or word hoard that all American poets have drawn on since. *Leaves of Grass* forms a Duden, without pictures, of the American language and as such it will always function as an ur-text for its poets. "To a Locomotive in Winter" is a thrilling example of how Whitman employs the diction of "golden brass and silvery steel . . . side-bars and connecting rods . . . springs and valves" to personify and humanize something mechanical to imbue a particular with his all-encompassing, inclusive, idiosyncratic, obsessive, modern sensibility. For Whitman, the "loveliness of Nature," to return to Wordsworth, was itself a "bar" to discovering "what in soul ye are," if it did not overwhelmingly include the "harsh" features of "Man's art."

In Radical Pursuit

A Brief Appreciation of the Essays of W. D. Snodgrass

"Our only hope as artists is to continually ask ourselves, 'Am I writing what I *really* think? Not what is acceptable; not what I wish I felt. Only what I cannot help thinking.'" This statement of artistic purpose is made by W. D. Snodgrass in "Finding a Poem," from his long-out-of-print book of essays, *In Radical Pursuit* (Harper and Row, 1974). Snodgrass has arranged the collection of twelve essays into three groups: "Four Personal Lectures," "Four Studies in the Moderns," and "Four Studies in the Classics." The classics Snodgrass takes up are *A Midsummer Night's Dream, Don Quixote, The Inferno,* and *The Iliad.* The section on moderns is less about individual works and more about issues of modernism approached by way of an essay each about Theodore Roethke, John Crowe Ransom, D. H. Lawrence, and Fyodor Dostoyevsky. The four personal lectures, "Tact and the Poet's Force," "Finding a Poem," "A Poem's Becoming," and "Poems About Paintings," pursue issues of craft and process in Snodgrass's own work.

Taken as a whole the collection is a helpful guide to understanding the underpinnings of Snodgrass's early work. All of the essays are fresh and lively, informed by the alacrity of Snodgrass's mind, which is genuinely eccentric and iconoclastic. All of the essays hew neatly to Snodgrass's requirement that artists write what they "really think." Reading them reminds one of how impoverished the art of the literary essay has become in the last two decades. Nevertheless, the brilliance of these essays is not the brilliance of original insight but the light shed by a mind deeply and passionately involved with its subject. As a result they are free of posturing and exist, primarily, to serve the subject at hand. Furthermore, they steer clear of what Snodgrass characterizes as "the shallower areas of the mind—such as artistic dogma and literary politics." His ambition for them is to settle in the "deeper and less conscious areas from which real creativity and discovery must come."

Woven throughout the collection is Snodgrass's conviction that the unconscious (a Freudian one, not surprisingly) provides access to the depths of creativity. This idea is most thoroughly expressed in the personal lectures. Again it is not the originality of his thought about the unconscious that is most interesting. What's truly interesting is the way it leads Snodgrass to talk about the development of his own work. In "Finding a Poem," Snodgrass reassembles the making of section 4 of "Heart's Needle," and in doing this he shows us how he uses form in the process of revision. It also helps bolster the not-well-enough-known fact that Snodgrass's very personal and direct poems were crucial influences in the development of Robert Lowell's *Life Studies* and "Confessional Poetry." The essay "Poems About Paintings" is a thorough examination, again, of Snodgrass's writing process. It is also one of the very early essays concerning what academics call ekphrastic poetry. Perhaps the most interesting essay in the entire collection is "Tact and the Poet's Force." In this piece, Randall Jarrell's poem "Protocols," which is about children arriving at the Birkenau concentration camp, is used to discuss the problem of handling details, especially extreme and disturbing details. Snodgrass claims that Jarrell by taking up his subject in an "understated" manner, "by avoiding melodramatic cliché," and "by showing [his] opponent's argument at its best" has found a way of re-creating the true horror of the children's dilemma, which is "not *how* people should kill children" but "that people *do* kill children." What's especially interesting about this essay is how it provides a rationale for Snodgrass's *Führer Bunker* poems. Snodgrass remarks at one point: "To write this poem (Jarrell's), you must first be willing to imagine yourself as a child in this situation—a *real* child. . . . Then, you must be willing to imagine yourself as a guard—this is the real test—and see how you would act. You must admit that moral weakness *could* lead you into such a position. . . . Until you are willing to admit you share some part of humanity's baseness and degradation, you cannot write about humanity's dignity and gentleness. Of all the ulterior motives, none is more common, none is more debilitating, none more damning than the pretense to moral superiority."

Jarrell is an apt model not only for "Tact and the Poet's Force," but he serves to show as well the league of writer with whom Snodgrass can comfortably be compared. Anyone who is not familiar with *In Radical Pursuit* and who wishes to understand the range of Snodgrass's mind and the intricacies of his concerns will do well to seek out this book from whichever libraries were wise enough to acquire it long ago.

Introduction to Annie Dillard's
Tickets for a Prayer Wheel

❧

IN 1974, WHEN ANNIE DILLARD was not quite twenty-nine years old, she published two books, almost simultaneously. The first was *Tickets for a Prayer Wheel,* a collection of poems with work dating back to the 1960s, and the second *Pilgrim at Tinker Creek,* a collection of essays written during the preceding eighteen months. *Tickets for a Prayer Wheel* had won the University of Missouri Press's "Break Away" publication prize for a first book of poems and within the year *Pilgrim at Tinker Creek* received the 1975 Pulitzer Prize for general nonfiction. *Pilgrim At Tinker Creek* was not an ordinary Pulitzer Prize–winning book. Its appearance quickly helped to give shape and direction to a developing tradition of late-twentieth-century American literary prose writers that includes Barry Lopez, John McPhee, Peter Mathiessen, Lewis Thomas, Terry Tempest Williams, and many others. In fact, Lewis Thomas's *The Lives of a Cell: Notes of a Biology Watcher,* which won the 1974 National Book Award, was published a few weeks after *Pilgrim at Tinker Creek.*

Given the privileged place prose holds in the American literary imagination and given the remarkable and deserved success of *Pilgrim at Tinker Creek,* it's not surprising that *Tickets for a Prayer Wheel,* even now, has received considerably less attention than her other work. This has occurred in spite of the fact that one of Dillard's publishers kept the book in print until recently. The oversight is unfortunate not only because *Tickets for a Prayer Wheel* contains a number of remarkable poems but because it offers Dillard readers an early glimpse at the passions and preoccupations that will make her one of America's most distinguished and distinctive writers. One of the passions the poems preview is her delight in uncovering illuminating facts about the physical world. Dillard once told an interviewer that she was interested "in the poetry of fact." When she tells us, in one of my favorite poems, "The Dominion of Trees," that "ground water walks / a mile a year," she uses a fact to create the leading edge of a metaphor about hidden forces at work in the earth. At times her preoccupations appear to run parallel, if not simultaneously, with *Pilgrim at Tinker Creek*. Thematically, both books address Thoreau's provocation: "With all your science can you tell how it is, and whence it is, that light comes into the soul?" And both books share information— "facts"—in a seamless manner, as if Dillard had been hunting for the proper form in which to fit them. In "The Dominion of Trees," she reports that "Falling from trees, / children accelerate / thirty-two feet / per second, per second." Likewise in *Pilgrim at Tinker Creek,* she imagines a mockingbird "accelerating thirty-two feet per second per second, through the empty air."

Readers coming to Annie Dillard's *Tickets for a Prayer Wheel* for the first time will find the book contains two types of poems: good but conventionally imagined short lyrics such as "The Clearing," "My Camel," and "The Shapes of Air," and longer meditative and speculative poems such as "Feast Days," "Bivouac," and "Tickets for a Prayer Wheel." The lyric with its compressions and elisions is congenial to Dillard's love of metaphor but overall I think it offers a container that's too small for her imagination. The longer meditative poems, however, are better suited to her temperament and its rangy enthusiasms. In "Bivouac," she is able to show how we carry with us a primal memory, or mythic consciousness, concerning our evolutionary journey from the sea. "You remember it all," Dillard writes, "how you lungless lay in slime, / how you shied across the plain / on your sharp split hoof, / the mist, the sip of ozone on the tongue." But memory is problematic because it can only provide partial, shadowy, dreamlike evidence of our origins and ultimately offers little consolation. We "wake" from this Darwinian-inflected dream to find we are on "the mainland" empowered with the "elephant eye" that keeps us alert to the present but mindful of mortality. "You die, you die," she reminds us unflinchingly. "First you go wet / and then you go dry." The sweep of a poem like "Bivouac" is early evidence of Dillard's ambition for herself as a literary artist. What one misses in the poems that is abundantly present in the prose is the acuity of perception—the "elephant eye"—by which Dillard delivers the arrow of her attention to the center of its target. Nevertheless, the poems contain abundant pleasures of their own like this prismatic experience in "The Dominion of Trees": "Lie in the dark, / shine a lantern up—/color! leaves still green."

Although it is probably true that many writers begin as poets, even if few ever publish their efforts, Dillard's *Tickets for a Prayer Wheel* could be considered as part of her almost congenital and ceaseless predisposition to explore new genres and themes. I can't think of a living American writer who has challenged herself so formidably in this way. By my count she has mastered the essay, memoir, literary criticism, novel, and autobiography to write about nature, theology, the creative process, memory, childhood, history, and more. Annie Dillard's capacious energy appears to have no limits and knows no bounds, which is why Wesleyan University Press's decision to reissue *Tickets for a Prayer Wheel* is good and timely. While Dillard keeps moving from literary bivouac to literary bivouac, to borrow one of her own resonate figures, the chance to consider her poems again allows those of us who are slower, less surefooted, less capable of providing for our own existential shelter, to look back over the remarkable "mainland" of experience she has assiduously explored for us and to locate her journey's origin in poetry. To discover that Annie Dillard is a poet at heart is less a discovery than an affirmation. Her work has always echoed the ancient and mysterious rhythms of the human breath. All of us pilgrims should be grateful for having these poems available again, for they can help to lead us back to our own beginnings, where we felt song rising out of us to start the prayer wheel turning.

Widow's Choice
Randall Jarrell's Letters

Randall Jarrell's Letters: An Autobiographical and Literary Selection, edited by Mary Jarrell, is a book of divided purposes that speaks to its readers through two voices, that of Randall Jarrell and that of his second wife, Mary. W. H. Auden believed that personal letters fell into two categories: "those in which the writer is in control of his situation—what he writes about is what he chooses to write—and those in which the situation dictates what he writes." Jarrell's voice is always in control of what he writes, because his voice is confident, self-searching, passionate, and honest. His voice is alive with those qualities that Robert Lowell, in a letter, once praised Jarrell for: "You stay young, and it's good to think of you, still so honest and hopeful and full of brilliant talk and knowledge, able to judge and make." Mary Jarrell's voice, on the other hand, which readers encounter in the many meticulous narrative passages inserted between letters, serves a noble but compromising purpose. She wishes to preserve and promote an image of her late husband that, while it reinforces those qualities cited by Lowell, is finally too narrow and guarded. It is an image that deliberately steers clear of honest discussion of the suicidal depression and domestic unhappiness that characterized the last few years of the poet's life. Fortunately, Randall Jarrell's direct and honest voice, writing about what he desires to write about, wins out over his wife's overprotective editing.

Randall Jarrell's Letters contains a wealth of information about one of the central voices of the generation of mid-twentieth-century poets that includes John Berryman, Elizabeth Bishop, Robert Lowell, and Delmore Schwartz. Until the appearance of these letters the only authoritative sources concerning Jarrell's life were the commemorative volume *Randall Jarrell, 1914–1965,* edited by Robert Lowell, Peter Taylor, and Robert Penn Warren, and several pieces written by Mary Jarrell. Much of the anecdotal material from the commemorative volume has been included in the narrative passages between letters and thus *Randall Jarrell's Letters* can serve as a short-form biography as well as a compendium of correspondence. However, if readers expect an "autobiography" as the subtitle suggests, their expectations will be frustrated by Mary Jarrell's control over much of the material.

The volume contains 350 letters culled from 2,500 considered by the editor. The first letter is by a twenty-one-year-old Jarrell writing to Robert Penn Warren about two poems Warren would use in the first issue of the *Southern Review* and about articles Jarrell was to write on Edna St. Vincent Millay and Auden. It concludes with a letter to a young Adrienne Rich to whom he exclaims, "How hard it is to write a good poem! How few good poems there are! What strange things you and I are, if we are. When we are! To have written one good poem . . ." The intervening five hundred–plus pages chronicle Jarrell's passionate search for and reverence of the "good" poem.

The search yields remarkable letters to Elizabeth Bishop, Robert Lowell, Adrienne Rich, and Karl Shapiro, to name a few. In them Jarrell advises, teases, criticizes, and encourages. To Robert Lowell, undecided about the direction his poetry should take after *The Mills of the Kavanaughs,* Jarrell coaches:

> Take a chance, Cal; let things work for you, if you've changed it will change the poems and in the long run change them for the good. I don't know whether this advice is right but I do know it's sincere, I go by it myself. I think you, less than any poet alive, need to worry about losing your style, your old way of doing things, enough of it will always be there no matter what you do.

When writing to Elizabeth Bishop about her poem "The Armadillo," he elevates her above her mentor Marianne Moore as well as himself:

> If my little foxes poem ("The Woman at the Washington Zoo") helped you with your armadillo poem, I'm awfully glad, because yours is ten times as good. They're all so good I hate to quote parts . . . Your poems seem really about real life, and to have as much of what's nice and beautiful and loving about the world as the world lets them have. I've quite got to like your poems better than Marianne Moore's as much as I like hers but life beats art, so to speak, and sense beats eccentricity, and the way things really are beats the most beautiful unreal visions, half-truths, one can fix up by leaving out and indulging oneself.

Exchanges such as these give credence to Lowell's claim that "Randall Jarrell was the only man I have ever met who could make other writers feel that their work was more important to him than his own."

Perhaps the most thoughtful letters in the collection are a series written to Adrienne Rich, whose second book, *The Diamond Cutters,* Jarrell had reviewed favorably. A five-page letter about Rich's *Snapshots of a Daughter- in-Law* provides a model of Jarrell's careful critical process. He tells her, "The poems seem like life first and poetry second, and have entirely lost any conventionally or traditionally poetic attitude." However, while praising her poems, he is not shy about telling her, "I thought 'arrows of light striking the water' maybe not as striking as it ought to be." Or "How glad I am that you're never influenced by Auden any more. He was bad for you, I thought." If there are places in the *Letters* where we feel Jarrell most relaxed and comfortable it is in his comments to his friends, such as Adrienne Rich, about their poems.

The letters are humorous and touching and delightful for what they reveal about Jarrell, such as his attempt to devote an entire chapter of his master's thesis at Vanderbilt to one of his own poems, a tactic he changed at the suggestion of his thesis advisor, Donald Davidson. We also see the young Jarrell slightly patronizing his mentors, especially Allen Tate. When Jarrell welcomes Allen Tate home to the South after Tate's three-year residency at Princeton, Jarrell calls the Northeast "that wretched direction."

When the letters aren't directly dealing with poetry, they are often concerned with books and ideas, or Jarrell's passion for opera and music or tennis and sports cars. Responding to Mary Jarrell about Louise Bogan's negative review of *The Seven-League Crutches,* Jarrell lampoons Bogan, imploring that "ere she perishes her girdle burst!" before going on to the shortcomings of the parking lights on a Nash-Healey Farina that he and Mary fantasize about owning.

When topical events enter the letters they do so in a characteristically concise and insightful way. Writing to Allen Tate after the death of Freud, Jarrell remarks, "I felt quite funny when Freud died, it was like having a continent disappear." In a letter to Robert Lowell, Jarrell mentions that he's upset about the dropping of the atomic bombs, and then again in a letter to Margaret Marshall, the literary editor of the *Nation,* on the same subject he says, "I feel so rotten about the country's response to the bombings of Hiroshima and Nagasaki that I wish I could become a naturalized dog or cat."

If Jarrell's wish to become a naturalized dog or cat sounds glib, we need only read a short way into the *Letters* to discover Jarrell's affection for animals. Of the seventeen letters selected from his correspondence to his first wife, Mackie, ten of them include references to their cat, Kitten. When Lowell's cat suffers an untoward event, Jarrell consoles his friend, "Anything happening to one's cat is the most painful subject in the world, so far as I'm concerned."

Although the letters themselves give a fair representation of Jarrell and his relationships to his contemporaries, the picture is not complete. Absent are Jarrell's letters to his best and oldest friend, Peter Taylor. Mary Jarrell explains that these letters were not made available to her, but offers no explanation. A glance at the index reveals there are more single-page references to Taylor than any other of Jarrell's friends including his wives and Robert Lowell. When Peter Taylor does appear it is in excerpts from his letters to Jarrell and in passages written by Mary Jarrell. These reconstructions, though welcomed, cannot replace the actual letters. Peter Taylor is not the only gap, however. Only one letter to John Berryman appears, yet Berryman in a tribute to Jarrell writes, "Our correspondence began in 1939." No letters to Robert Fitzgerald are reprinted either, yet Mary Jarrell pieces together the details of their long friendship. It is hard to imagine that Jarrell's letters to these friends are just not very interesting. Jarrell found the task of writing letters laborious, and he would not have written idly or frivolously to such significant friends. Berryman's and Fitzgerald's stature requires fuller representation in this volume, especially since Mary Jarrell includes their names in the dedication to the book, or a better explanation about their absence.

The absence of important letters from the volume indicates a larger problem with the collection: Mary Jarrell's overwhelming presence. In her preface she states that "just as Freud's and Mozart's letters speak of Freud and Mozart, Jarrell's letters are Jarrell," and although this is the kind of self-evident statement few would argue with, it becomes clear as we read the *Letters* that yes, this is Jarrell, but a Jarrell arranged and edited in such a way that promotes Mary Jarrell's cherished version of her husband. Absent from the *Letters* is that side of Jarrell that some of his friends describe as "lonely but faintly monstrous," "difficult, touchy and oversensitive," and "formidable and bristling."

Mary Jarrell's desire to fashion a particular image of her husband is not an unpardonable sin. It is understandable that as his widow she would want to choose those letters that would show her husband in the best light, but twenty years have passed since Jarrell was killed by a car and we are still no closer to learning the truth about his death. The facts remain unclear as to whether Jarrell, out for an evening walk in Chapel Hill, North Carolina, where he was undergoing physical therapy at the Memorial Hospital Hand Clinic, was sideswiped by an oncoming car or if he threw himself into its path, as the driver claimed. By refusing to entertain the possibility that her husband killed himself, she calls more attention to the murky circumstances of his demise.

The matter of Jarrell's death is not the only area of his life she sanitizes. In the July–August, 1977 issue of the *American Poetry Review*, she published portions of a correspondence between Jarrell and a young Austrian ceramicist Elisabeth Eisler, whom Jarrell met in 1948 while he was lecturing in Salzburg at the American Seminars. At the time Jarrell was married to his first wife, Mackie, and he had recently concluded a year teaching at Sarah Lawrence and working as the literary editor of the *Nation*. In presenting the letters, Mary Jarrell is vague about the nature of the relationship between Jarrell and Elisabeth Eisler. A reader might suppose it is either a rather intense teacher-student friendship or a romantic platonic one. But when we read these same letters assembled in the present volume, we learn a number of interesting facts about the relationship that Mary Jarrell originally omitted. Left out from the *American Poetry Review* article is the fact that Jarrell and Ms. Eisler exchanged seventy letters, most of them during the fall of 1949. In one letter Jarrell confesses, "I can't be anyone's husband but yours." In the *APR* selection, Mary Jarrell's silent editing of passages and the restructuring of paragraphs skew the picture of the relationship between Eisler and Jarrell. In the *APR* version of one letter we find:

> I work hard at poetry but put off or don't do many other things: I hate even the feeling of having lots of little duties even if they're quite easy ones.

and in the *Letters* version:

> I work hard at poetry but put off or don't DO, many other things; I hate even the feeling of having lots of little duties, even if they're quite easy ones—so, I'm not as much help to my wife as I should be, though I may be up to the European average; I don't know, I doubt it.

And then again from the same letter in the *APR* version:

> I lead an odd independent social [*sic*] life remarkably unlike most other people's lives, the life of someone whose principal

work and amusement is writing and reading and thinking about things. I like the feeling of being taken care of . . .

And in the *Letters* version:

> I lead an odd, independent, unsocial life remarkably unlike most other people's lives, the life of someone whose principal work-and-amusement is writing, and reading and thinking about things. And this isn't nice for one's wife unless she has some great interest to take up most of her time.

The deleted phrases themselves may sound rather insignificant, but the fact that Mary Jarrell changed paragraphing and punctuation, and deleted only references to Mackie shows how sensitive she is about Jarrell's image as a husband. The restoration of the deleted material to the Austrian letters in the present volume does not make us worry any less about her editorial objectivity. We wouldn't expect Mary Jarrell to belabor the details of her husband's extramarital affairs, even though the affair predates her marriage to him, but readers do deserve to be told something of the importance of Elisabeth Eisler in Jarrell's life. Jarrell was impossibly in love with Elisabeth Eisler and was inspired by phrases and images contained in her letters, phrases and images which found their way into poems, such as "Orient Express," one of his most highly regarded poems.

To her credit Mary Jarrell provides a fuller context for the Austrian letters in the present volume and allows us to see that her husband's relationship with Elisabeth Eisler was more intimate than the *APR* selection indicated. Even so she cannot keep herself from coloring and distorting Jarrell's life. This is especially true when it comes to the letters Jarrell wrote to her. Of the one hundred letters Mary possesses from him, she has included seventy-three. Several of these letters could have been fairly traded for a John Berryman or Robert Fitzgerald letter. As it is, in the face of Jarrell's controversial death and the difficulties that Mary and he went through during the last few years of his life, the letters are piled up like evidence to prove that not only did Jarrell love his wife, but he loved her best. This creates an imbalance in the story the *Letters* tell and it also reveals Mary Jarrell's insecurity about the place she held in Jarrell's life at the end.

Concerning the inclusion of these love letters, Mary Jarrell tells us, "As with the Eisler letters, only the most literary and autobiographical portions . . . have been excerpted and presented, with occasional small deletions made silently." Because of our knowledge of the deletions made to the Eisler letters in *APR,* we can only wonder about the "small deletions made silently" in her own letters. Many readers have waited a long time for the publication of *Randall Jarrell's Letters,* hoping they would clarify the mysteries that surround the illness and chaos of his last years, but although they give us much that is new and interesting concerning his poetry and friendships, we learn very little about his manic-depressive states, his suicide attempt, or his reasons for wanting to divorce Mary. Instead, in her preface, Mary Jarrell refers to her husband's trouble as a "mid-life crisis." She uses the phrase in such a way that it suggests Jarrell used it himself, yet there is no evidence for this in the volume. Characterizing the emotional confusion and physical illness that wrecked Jarrell from 1963 to 1965 as a "midlife crisis" diminishes the painful experiences that he suffered and worked hard to overcome.

The place that Mary Jarrell's version can be least trusted is in her explanation of her husband's death. It is not in her interest to go any further into the details of her husband's problems than she needs, and especially to go no further than to suggest that his mental illness and wrist-slashing episode were aberrations from which he fully recovered before his accidental death. The last seven years of Jarrell's life are represented with less than sixty letters, many of which are written to Michael Di Capua, Jarrell's friend and editor. We do learn that Jarrell found it difficult to write letters as he got older, but to have so few during this least-known and most controversial period of his life creates a gap more conspicuous than the absence of letters from Berryman, Fitzgerald, and Taylor. Because so few letters speak for these years, a reader is once again in the awkward position of having to trust Jarrell's defensive widow. This defensiveness reveals itself most clearly in her narrative passages. In one such passage, she reports that Jarrell's orthopedist prescribed intensive physical therapy for the peripheral nerve damage his hand suffered as a result of his suicide attempt. Plans were made to admit Jarrell to the Hand Clinic of the University of North Carolina Medical School when space was available. Mary Jarrell ends the passage with the unexplained remark, "A skin graft was not considered." Although Mary Jarrell does not clarify the otherwise vague reference to a skin graft, she means to address critics, such as Jeffrey Meyers, who insist that Jarrell entered the hospital to undergo physical therapy and a skin graft to cover the scar of his self-inflicted wound. Unfortunately, instead of taking the opportunity to address Myers' claim directly, she refers to it obliquely.

One of the most revealing details about Mary Jarrell's attitude toward her husband's death is the way she conflates her description of the death of Jarrell's beloved cat, Kitten, with her husband's. "One night," she writes, "he (Kitten) didn't come home. Kitten was hit at the side of the road by a car. . . . One blow on his skull killed him instantly. . . . The beautiful eyes and face, and the graceful body were not hurt in any way." In an earlier published memoir, "A Group of Two," Mary Jarrell directly compared the manner of Kitten's demise with her husband's. "Like Randall," she writes in "A Group of Two," "one blow on his [Kitten's] skull killed him instantly. Again like Randall, the beautiful eyes and face, and the graceful body were not hurt in any way."

Perhaps because of the autopsy report that has recently come to light describing Jarrell's terrible wounds and gashes, Mary Jarrell decided to tone down the melodramatic version of her husband's death. If so, it didn't prevent her from doing a cut-and-paste job on the newspaper account of his death. From the newspaper article we learn that "the impact of the car spun Jarrell around and knocked him not more than three or four feet to the side." The coroner reports that he was "hit from the side, not from the front, or the wheels." This is valuable information, but it does not answer why one of the occupants in the automobile that struck Jarrell testified, "He seemed to whirl," and he "lunged into the path of the car." In an effort to refute the eyewitness account, Mary Jarrell concludes that had her husband lunged he would have been run over, "but that was not the case." It might well be true that if Jarrell had lunged he would have been run over, but whirling and lunging could just as easily have produced the side-swipe that injured him only on the left side.

Finally, Mary Jarrell's version of Jarrell's death is not very convincing. However, it is consistent with her past attempts to fashion the image of a husband who is good and faithful and who even lying dead by the side of the road could have beautiful eyes and a graceful body, who seemed to be asleep rather than contused and bleeding. Or one who could have a passionate exchange of letters with a younger woman without being in any way unfaithful to his first wife. This coloring of Jarrell's life, this beatification, makes *Randall Jarrell's Letters* less useful as a biography than it could have been, and unfortunately it does little to clarify questions about his tragic death. For readers who wish neither to sensationalize nor romanticize Randall Jarrell, Mary Jarrell's presence in the *Letters* is frustrating. On the other hand, the *Letters* represents an invaluable resource for those who believe Randall Jarrell wrote some of the most enduring poems of his time and that the future will see a rise in his stature and will profess an ever increasing wonderment and astonishment for his work.

The Wesleyan Tradition

❦

MY FIRST ENCOUNTER with the Wesleyan poetry program took place more than twenty years ago in Arizona at the main branch of the Phoenix Public Library. Books by James Dickey, James Wright, Louis Simpson, Robert Bly, David Ignatow, Philip Levine, and Donald Justice had already been well-used by the time I began taking them home, for two-week furloughs, in 1971. A nineteen-year-old, with three semesters of college, who was trying to imagine a literary life for himself in the middle of what was just then being called the Sunbelt, I had no way of appreciating the significance of these books. The poems of Wright, Bly, Dickey, Levine, and Simpson were unlike anything I had ever read. Simpson's "American Poetry," with its "stomach that can digest / Rubber, coal, uranium, moons, poems" and its humorous "shark" that "contains a shoe" and utters "cries that are almost human," was typical of the forceful immediacy and urgency I felt when reading the early Wesleyan poets. It was an urgency that was carried beyond the first-decade poets and into the seventies, and could be heard in James Wright's "I am almost afraid to write down / This thing," which begins "The Old WPA Swimming Pool in Martins Ferry, Ohio." As a group what these poets seemed most "afraid" of was a vision of America they could not turn away from. This vision demanded, as James Dickey wrote, that we witness "not just the promise, not just the loss and the 'betrayal of the American ideal/the Whitmanian ideal' . . . but the whole 'complex fate,' the difficult and agonizing meaning of being an American, of living as an American at the time in which one chances to live" (75). The whole "complex fate" was that penchant in the American character that could produce, as James Wright noted, "so many things . . . that begin nobly and end meanly" ("The Delicacy of Walt Whitman," 4). If the form of these poems was unfamiliar to me—freer, more open than high-school textbook poetry though calmer and less inchoate than the Ginsberg and Ferlinghetti I had read—their description of America and of what it meant to be an American was not unfamiliar. In a pure and direct way these poets made it clear to me that the struggle to make sense of one's life through poetry is a struggle, on one level, with form.

These poets also demonstrated that poetry was connected to the larger cultural forces and changes taking place within American society. It spoke of dying cities, of the solitude and isolation of the suburbs, of the size of the country, of the Vietnam War, of immigrants, of the middle and working classes, as it carried the "news" all Americans needed to hear about their country. In the broadest sense many of the early Wesleyan poets represented the democratization of poetry that was taking place through the creative writing programs in American universities and colleges. Justice, Levine, Donald Petersen, and William Dickey, all early Wesleyan poets, had been members of the same poetry-writing workshop at the University of Iowa in the mid-fifties. The tie, though not a causal one, between the Wesleyan poetry program and creative writing programs would remain strong and influential throughout the decades. As a result of this connection, the early Wesleyan books not only contained an aesthetic for beginning writers like me, but they also proved that poetry and the universities had an implicit institutional relationship and that even while many early Wesleyan poets rebelled against the Academic and institutionalized poetry of New Criticism, the rebellion was taking place, so to speak, within the palace. This is not to say that poets such as Bly, Wright, James Dickey, Simpson, and Levine did little to change the kind of poetry being written in America. On the contrary, poetry and the writing of poetry had become an activity of phenomenal proportions in the seventies, eighties, and nineties because of the profound effect the early Wesleyan poets had on the narrow dominant aesthetic of the fifties. The history of these changes, the history of this phenomenon, can be seen in the Wesleyan poetry program. No other university or commercial press poetry list can provide as wide a view or as broad a history of contemporary American poetry as can the Wesleyan list, and in this way *The Wesleyan Tradition: Four Decades of American Poetry* stands as a definitive record of American poetry written since the late fifties.

Providing a record or survey of such a distinguished tradition carries an obvious significance, but as a reader of this anthology I would be impatient if a record or survey were the limit of the anthology's accomplishment. The central role occupied by the Wesleyan poetry program during the last four decades of American poetry offers a unique opportunity to assess not only the poetry program but also contemporary American poetry since 1959. Furthermore, as an assessment the anthology implicitly places the tradition of Wesleyan poetry within the broader changes taking place in American culture, so that a reader can see not only what kinds of poems are representative of the Wesleyan poetry program but also gain an understanding of why such poems were written.

When I first discovered the Wesleyan Poets, in 1971, the program had already exceeded its first decade. An anthology entitled *Decade: A Collection of Poetry from the First Ten Years of The Wesleyan Poetry Program,* edited by Norman Holmes Pearson, had been published in 1969. In his introduction to the anthology, Pearson remarked that at the start of the program, in the late fifties, "Somehow the publishing of poetry, though not the writing of it, had been in the doldrums. The Wesleyan series helped to stir the air." The immediate model for the program came from the Yale University Press Yale Series of Younger Poets, which since 1919 had been publishing first books of poems by poets under the age of forty. Except for Yale poets Muriel Rukeyser, Paul Engle, James Agee, William Meredith, and Eve Merriam, the Yale Series, in thirty years, had done little to distinguish itself, until W. H.

Auden became its editor in 1950. Auden's decade of editorship yielded Adrienne Rich, W. S. Merwin, John Ashbery, James Wright, John Hollander, and William Dickey. Auden demonstrated that the institutional support of a university press combined with a strong editorial vision could produce a distinguished poetry list. All of Auden's choices, except perhaps Ashbery, were committed to writing exemplary and distinctive Academic poetry in which technique, surface, literary allusion, artifice, and compression were highly valued. This style, a product of late-modern, New Critical attitudes, prized distance and control, objectivity and irony as poetry's highest achievements. Academic poetry flourished, as Robert Von Hallberg has pointed out, in the "decade after the war" when there had been "a demand in America for those signs of cultural coherence that help to ratify [the] imperium" (28). The cultural coherence of the Academic poets came not so much from American culture as it did from the English tradition of lyric poetry, filtered through the New Criticism of John Crowe Ransom, Allen Tate, Yvor Winters, and Robert Penn Warren. In the late forties and fifties the Academic style had been given a lively embodiment through the work of Richard Wilbur. Acknowledging the pervasiveness of Wilbur's influence, Randall Jarrell once noted, in an address to the Library of Congress on the state of American poetry, "There is another larger group of poets who, so to speak, came out from under Richard Wilbur's overcoat."

Richard Wilbur was teaching at Wesleyan University at the time Willard Lockwood formed Wesleyan University Press in 1958. Lockwood, as the first director of the Press, and Wilbur, as an advisor, decided to commit part of the energy of the new press to publishing contemporary poetry. As outlined on the dust-jacket copy of early books, "The purpose of The Wesleyan Poetry Program is to publish regularly collections of outstanding contemporary poetry in English. Manuscripts are welcomed from anyone. They are read by the distinguished poets and critics who comprise the especial editorial board that makes publishing recommendations. There are no restrictions on form or of style. The Program attempts, quite simply, to publish the best poetry written today. Its single criterion of acceptance is excellence."

Donald Hall, William Meredith, and Norman Holmes Pearson were the members of the first poetry editorial board. The original intention of the program was to bring out, simultaneously, hardback and paperback editions of four books each year. The first four poets represented were Barbara Howes, Hyam Plutzik, Louis Simpson, and James Wright. The books met with critical success and the new publishing venture was praised as a model for future university press poetry programs. In the decades that followed, the number of books the program published annually varied, from as few as four to as many as sixteen, and the editorial board rotated its membership.

In the aftermath of Wesleyan's success approximately fifteen university press poetry series were established. Along with the Wesleyan program these have filled a gap left in the publication of poetry by the indifference of the commercial presses. In his preface to *Vital Signs: Contemporary American Poetry from the University Presses,* Ronald Wallace quotes David Wojahn on the importance of the university press poetry series: "Nearly thirty years after Wesleyan started its poetry series, poetry has been more defined and shaped by the university press than by the commercial or small house" (29). Although many of the early Wesleyan poets had published first books before coming to the program, the majority were first-book poets. The history of the Wesleyan University Press poetry program demonstrates that Wesleyan was often a starting place for poets who, once their reputations were made, moved on to commercial houses. This springboard aspect is an inherent feature of many university press poetry programs. Recently, however, Wesleyan has welcomed back a number of its early authors, James Dickey, David Ignatow, and Harvey Shapiro, as well as provided a place for midcareer poets such as Gregory Orr, Heather McHugh, Rachel Hadas, Sherod Santos, and Donald Revell. In the almost thirty-five years since Wesleyan began filling the publishing gap of poetry, that gap has become the most real and significant territory for mainstream American poetry.

Although many university presses followed Wesleyan's lead as a publisher of poetry, Wesleyan's method of selecting its manuscripts remained distinctive. Most university press poetry programs have relied on a single editor or an individual guest judge to make editorial recommendations. Wesleyan's "especial editorial board" of poets and critics helped keep the Wesleyan program alive to the widest possibilities of the newest work being written.

The method at times made it possible for individual board members to lobby hard for special interests without having to take responsibility for the long-term features of the program. Consensus as an editorial policy also led to some regrettable decisions. Wesleyan had published Philip Levine's very successful first full-length collection, *Not This Pig,* but when be submitted *They Feed They Lion,* the board turned it down, twice. In the Press's file on the decision, the brief comments by the board record that two of the readers were largely in favor of Levine's manuscript, but that the third member, who strongly opposed it, was able to sway the other two.

On the surface the incident involving Levine's *They Feed They Lion* might appear to be the result of an editorial decision reached through consensus, but it also signaled the aesthetic limits the program would rarely venture beyond. Levine's *Not This Pig* is emotionally direct and unrelenting in its indictment of capitalist America; nevertheless, it has manners, rhyme and meter; it behaves itself. But *They Feed They Lion,* though it uses rhetoric skillfully (the title poem could not be more highly cadenced and controlled), also projects the scary anarchy that broke through the surface of the "imperium" of mannered America during the era of inner-city race riots and antiwar demonstrations of the sixties. *They Feed They Lion* represented what the establishment poets of the fifties could be said to have feared most, disintegration of the cultural fabric of American life and disavowal of the modes of poetic discourse they had labored to justify. The decision not to publish Levine's second book is typical of the decisions that throughout its history has kept the Wesleyan program solidly within the mainstream and normative in contemporary American poetry. But in light of these limits, it is important to underscore that the early Wesleyan board, especially in Wilbur, Meredith, Hall, Pearson, and Hollander, showed generosity and foresight in understanding aesthetics antagonistic to their own. The ability of the early board members to identify the best poets of a rebellious generation allowed the Wesleyan poetry program to take advantage of larger and more far-reaching changes taking place within American culture. This ability, more than anything else, is what established the program's reputation.

The creation of the Wesleyan program profited from this period of vigor and confidence in America's poetry. This confidence came from a common sense of purpose at the center of American culture, a sense of purpose buoyed by the postwar boom and expansion, regardless of the ominous shadows cast by McCarthyism and the Korean "conflict." Robert Von Hallberg writes that American poets of the fifties were confident of being in "the honorable tradition of addressing the audience that felt greatest responsibility for the refinement of taste and the preservation of a national culture" (34). The fact that the mainstream culture was so well defined and, in Von Hallberg's words, "effective at dominating cultural institutions" (35) provided the resistance that gave rise to an avant-garde. Although the early Wesleyan poets were hardly members of the fifties avant-garde (the Beats and Black Mountaineers), their poetry was stubbornly committed to finding new forms of expression. Both the Beats and the early Wesleyan poets had taken up Walt Whitman's democratic ideas about poetry. Although each group would exploit different aspects of the great poet for their own, their interest in Whitman revealed a common desire to reinvent American poetry.

At the same time that changes were taking place in mainstream American poetry, the institutions that had supported this poetry were changing as well. The system of American land-grant universities was expanding rapidly. Graduate creative writing programs on the model of the Iowa Writers' Workshop proliferated. The English departments, which had given homes to professor poets such as Ransom, Tate, Blackmur, Winters, and Warren, were now host to poet professors who took the New Critical approaches of the previous generation and adapted them to their creative writing workshops. By looking at the evolving connection between universities, poets, and publishing, it is easy to surmise that a program such as Wesleyan's arrived to meet the future publishing needs of university creative writing programs.

From a larger cultural perspective what was happening in contemporary American poery began to resemble Tocqueville's description of the literary arts in a democratic society. In *Democracy in America* Tocqueville wrote: "Taken as a whole literature in democratic ages can never represent, as it does in the periods of aristocracy, an aspect of order, regularity, science, and art; its form will, on the contrary, ordinarily be slighted, sometimes despised. Style will frequently be fantastic, incorrect, overburdened, and loose—almost always vehement and bold. Authors will aim at rapidity of execution, more than at perfection of detail. . . . The object of authors will be to astonish rather than to please, and to stir the passions more than to stir the taste." Tocqueville was responding to, and in fact lamenting, the expansion of the cultural center in democratic ages—art and poetry, the aesthetic taste, emerging from individuals and constituencies as consensus rather than from cathedrals and courts. For poetry in particular this widening cultural center meant that the traditional geographical hubs for poetry, such as New York, Boston, and, since the Second World War, San Francisco, would expand to include colleges and universities located in places like Iowa City, Fresno, Minneapolis, Ann Arbor, and Black Mountain.

From within the circle of establishment and Academic poets, the widening of the American cultural center was not yet so apparent. In his acceptance speech for the National Book Award in 1960 Robert Lowell described the two major camps in American poetry as "raw" and "cooked." This simplified matters, and took the important differences between the poets represented in Donald Allen's *The New American Poetry* (1960) and Donald Hall, Robert Pack, and Louis Simpson's *New Poets of England and America* (1957) at face value. It also had the effect of reducing aesthetic distinctions to matters of table manners and cultural nutrition and ignored the deeper changes that had taken place. The confidence that allowed establishment poets of the fifties, including Lowell, to see themselves as upholders of a universal American literary taste began to crumble, however, as the institutional structures of publishing and education shifted and broadened their bases. But perhaps the larger reason for the breakdown in confidence was that American culture as a whole had begun to question the domestic and foreign policies of its government. The pressures that the Beat and Black Mountain poets had put on the Academic poets throughout the fifties was no longer coming from the periphery of the culture but radiated from the center as well. The Wesleyan poetry program took advantage of the changes occurring in mainstream American poetry by establishing a publishing enterprise suited to the democratization of art and culture that had begun in the fifties and would continue to accelerate over the next three decades.

The Sixties

In his 1963 essay "A Wrong Turning in American Poetry" Robert Bly wrote, "Our recent poetry is [also] a poetry in which the poem is considered to be a construction independent of the poet. It is imagined that when the poet says 'I' in a poem he does not mean himself, but rather some other person—'the poet'—a dramatic hero. The poem is conceived as a clock which one sets going. This idea encourages the poet to construct automated and flawless machines. Such poems have thousands of intricately moving parts, dozens of iambic belts and pulleys, precision trippers that rhyme at the right moment, lights flashing alternately red and green, steam valves that whistle like birds." Bly's attack on American poetry is aimed both at the Academic verse of the period—with its emphasis on conventions, manner, and decorum instead of feeling, spontaneity, and sincerity—as well as at the Black Mountain poets who by focusing so heavily on William Carlos Williams had fostered, in

Bly's words, an "American isolationism" born of the "American-ism of material, words, meter, and attitude as subjects for poetry" ("Words of Robert Creeley," 13). Both kinds of poetry had deval-ued the "image," which Bly believed was modernism's most significant achievement. Bly wanted poetry to return to the early roots of modernism and to the energy and innovation of the gen-eration of 1917 which had found its most expressive and impor-tant homes in European and Latin American poetry. Besides his concern for the image, Bly criticized American poetry for its nine-teenth-century obsession with "technique." "When poets talk of technique," Bly wrote in his well-known essay "Looking for Dragon Smoke," "they are usually headed for jail." In general, Bly, Wright, Simpson, Dickey, and Ignatow believed that imagery grew out of the spontaneous and associative activities of the imagina-tion which would give them unguarded access to the world of the unconscious. The image was the key to unlocking the door of the psyche, both collective and individual, behind which lay the truth of one's experience. Bly's method, which dominated American poetry for more than a decade, was supposed to release the image "from imprisonment among objects." Such a release, Bly wrote at the end of "A Wrong Turning in American Poetry," would have the curative effect of freeing American culture from its "technical obsession" and of reversing the dark processes "of business men-tality, of human effort dissipated among objects, of expansion, of a destructive motion outward."

Bly provided the most passionate critical voice for a school that became known as Deep Imagism. If at times Bly's criticism was hectoring and contradictory, it was unequivocal about the direc-tion in which mainstream American poetry was headed, away from the enervated verse of the academy with its reticence and manners, good sense and equilibrium, stricture and restraint, toward an open, more inclusive, democratic, and associative poetry that produced what critics later called the "emotive imagi-nation." Although "A Wrong Turning in American Poetry" was published in 1963, it described changes that had begun to take place in American poetry during the fifties.

Bly's claim for the "image" was large, but it was not the only new claim for poetry being made in America. Charles Olson published his essay "Projective Verse" in 1950. Ginsberg had given his first public reading of *Howl* in 1954. John Ashbery's *Some Trees* appeared in 1956. Frank O'Hara's mock manifesto "Personism" and Robert Lowell's *Life Studies* were both published in 1959.

Perhaps the most important group that arose in the fifties was that of the confessional poets. Robert Lowell, Sylvia Plath, W. D. Snodgrass, John Berryman, and Anne Sexton had been schooled in Academic verse and throughout their careers retained an allegiance to formal poetry. But the confessional poets used convention and form as scaffolding on which to hang the seemingly unvarnished facts of the poet's often dramatic and tragic life. In confessional poetry the distance between the poet and the poem disappeared. Autobiography replaced history. For the early Wesleyan poets, the confessional mode represented a way in which to speak with sincerity and honesty about what mattered most.

The confessional poets also had the important effect of being models of passionate if not reckless living for younger poets. Philip Levine has provided an example of such a model in a memoir about John Berryman as a teacher at the Iowa Writers' Workshop in 1954. "These were among the darkest days of the Cold War," Levine writes, "and yet John was able to convince us— merely because he believed it so deeply—that nothing could be more important for us, for the nation, for humankind, than our becoming the finest poets we could become" (541). This unswerving personal commitment to poetry, to one's art, became an important part of the atmosphere of creative writing workshops where the vocabulary for discussing poetry began to include more expressive or emotive terms, so that young poets were encouraged to "take risks," or insure their poems had "earned the right" to say what they were saying.

Whereas Deep Image poetry freed poets to explore the unseen and invisible, to confront the convolutions of the psyche, confessional poetry, either by directly using the material of one's life or through personae, permitted poets to dramatize their personal experience. Early Wesleyan poets such as Simpson, James Dickey, Levine, Richard Howard, as well as James Wright and Bly to some extent, all became actors in their own poems. There was a freshness in writing such as Levine's "The Cemetery at Academy, California": "On a hot summer Sunday / I came here with my children / who wandered among headstones / kicking up dust clouds." Or in Dickey's "The Performance": "The last time I saw Donald Armstrong / He was staggering oddly off into the sun, / Going down, of the Philippine Islands."

But the history of the Wesleyan University Press poetry program's first decade is not only a history of innovation and revolution; it is also a history of the waning influence of those poets who, in Jarrell's phrase, had come out from under Wilbur's overcoat. Vassar Miller, Robert Bagg, Donald Petersen, W. R. Moses, David Ferry, and Barbara Howes all produced an interesting and distinctive poetry. In David Ferry's "My Parents en Route," for example, a haunting dream portrait of his parents "catafalqued" asleep in their beds is created by Ferry's consummate handling of formal devices. Donald Petersen, in "Ballad of Dead Yankees," gives life to an old convention through the boldness and near absurdity of the poem's subject:

> Where's the swagger, where's the strut?
> Where's the style that was the hitter?
> Where's the pitcher's swanlike motion?
> What in God's name turned life bitter?

Audaciousness and formal skill are also evident in what I like to think of as Alan Ansen's quirky and beautiful "vanishing" sestina, "A Fit of Something Against Something," which also satirizes the claims of free verse:

> New rebels will not master
> Forms pointlessly austere.
> They feel they will be
> Screwed by that alien order,

That Gestapo sestina,
Cats, it's the most ungone.

The end of the first decade of the Wesleyan program marks the end of its period of greatest influence on American poetry. Wright, Bly, Levine, Justice, Dickey, Simpson, Ignatow, Howard, and Ashbery all left the Press for commercial publishers. The seventies and following decades of the program would be devoted primarily to publishing poets influenced by the work of the first-decade Wesleyan poets.

The Seventies

The end of a decade of experimentation and rebellion from within the mainstream of American poetry coincided with a general flattening of cultural energy in the country. A highly conventional Deep Image or surreal poem had emerged, as empty and predictable in its concerns as the Academic poem, which it replaced, had been in the fifties. By 1971 parodies of Deep Imagism such as Harvey Shapiro's friendly but pointed "Hello There!" began to appear, and an impatience from critics and poets concerning the opacity of Deep Imagism could be found in essays and reviews of contemporary poetry.

HELLO THERE!
for Robert Bly

The poets of the midwest
Are in their towns,
Looking out across wheat, corn,
Great acres of silos.
Neruda waves to them
From the other side of the field.
They are all so happy
They make images.

Bly's influence wasn't limited to a kind of "happy," ham-fisted, poet-in-overalls, image-making, however. His magazine *The*

Fifties, and then *The Sixties,* along with *kayak* and *Lillabulero* helped to establish and promote a serious and influential tradition of surrealism in contemporary American poetry. Outside the Wesleyan program Mark Strand, W. S. Merwin, Bill Knott, Charles Simic, and William Matthews had developed styles in the surrealist mode. Except perhaps for Matthews, these poets produced image-based poems quite different from the kind that Bly and Wright produced. In 1973 Paul Zweig, in an essay entitled "The New Surrealism," noted that Bly's Deep Imagism "is more concerned with spiritual exploration than with surreal language. His plea for 'imagery,' and against traditional rhetoric, brings him closer to Rilke, Vallejo, and Neruda, than to the provocations of Breton." This division between the spiritual side of Deep Imagism and the more intellectual and "shocking" side of a purer surrealism is played out among several Wesleyan poets of the seventies. Russell Edson, Michael Benedikt, and James Tate, with their absurd and mischievous sense of humor, their fractured fables for the imagination, and their emphasis on surface, are much closer to the linguistic attitudes of Breton. The Wesleyan poets most faithful to Bly's "spiritual exploration" are John Haines and Vern Rutsala. Rutsala in his prose poems and Haines in his short lyrics represent classical deep image concerns about the dark, mysterious regions and dreamscape of the unconscious.

The Wesleyan poet who found a way to bring both the spiritual and linguistic sides of surrealism together was Charles Wright. "The New Poem," published in his second Wesleyan book, *Hard Freight* (1973), represents a kind of High Deep Imagism or High New Surrealism:

> It will not resemble the sea.
> It will not have dirt on its thick hands.
> It will not be part of the weather.
>
> It will not reveal its name.
> It will not have dreams you can count on.
> It will not be photogenic.

It will not attend our sorrow.
It will not console our children.
It will not be able to help us.

During the seventies, as Charles Wright published four books with Wesleyan, he developed away from the High Deep Imagism of "The New Poem" and its minimalist emotional scale. Yet he has remained a poet for whom the image, which he builds upon with a lavish and obsessive care, is still the most powerful and basic unit of poetic construction.

If the freshness and originality that had marked the innovations in American poetry during the sixties had become conventions by the seventies, so too had some of the features of university press poetry publishing. The concept of a poetry series had spread to commercial houses such as Houghton Mifflin and George Braziller and in the late seventies to Alfred A. Knopf. As a result the Wesleyan poetry program found itself in competition not only with other university presses but with commercial houses as well. The poetry lists at Atheneum and at Farrar, Straus and Giroux had expanded in the sixties and boasted some of the best recognized and original poets. This competition made it more difficult for Wesleyan to attract or keep, perhaps even to identify, the best poets of the next generation. While the seventies at Wesleyan produced many fine and distinguished poets, the overall profile of the decade is first-book poets, working deftly in the period style.

That a period style in surrealism and the Deep Image developed so rapidly in American poetry of the sixties is an indication not only of the need for a new direction in poetry but also of the influence of creative writing programs. Cataloging the diction of Deep Imagism in 1974 ("breath," "snow," "future," "blood," "silence," "eats," "water") Robert Pinsky noted, "somewhere, on some campus in America, a young poet is writing a sentence with all or nearly all of the totemic words" of surrealistic diction (165). At its most conventional and formulaic, this writing was made for the democracy of the classroom. It stubbornly resisted traditional prosody, was brief, and could be handled with the expressive critical vocabulary of the workshop. This style, which Pinsky dubbed "one-of-the-guys surrealism," possessed the migratory habits of American culture as well, and, in spite of Shapiro's "poets of the midwest," the surrealist diction was as comfortable in the city as on the farm, in Tucson as Ann Arbor.

But Pinsky discovered a relative health in the poetry of America and like Bly, though without Bly's proselytizing, called for a change in the kind of poem being written. Pinsky found surrealist and Deep Imagist poems limited because they trusted "perception . . . more . . . than reflection," and eschewed ideas because they were "obstacles" to discovering the "large, blank, irreducible phenomena" that were, to surrealists, the "truest incarnations of reality" (165). Pinsky asked that poets return to more expansive forms, to take up meditative and discursive modes, and to exploit the "prose virtues" of poetry.

Pinsky's reading of American poetry in the mid-seventies is particularly relevant to this anthology because he uses a number of Wesleyan poets to make his case concerning the possibilities of post–Deep Imagism and American surrealist poetry. For Pinsky, James Wright's "Two Poems about President Harding" is an exception to the surrealist rule of producing "blank, irreducible phenomenon." Wright's poem, according to Pinsky, reveals the "unsuspected, essential parts of the invisible web of thoughts covering the world" (166). The revelation of this web is something that Pinsky believes is usually dependent upon "a rather proselike, sensible context or frame" (166). As an example of a poem with a "sensible context or frame," Pinsky offers "The Soldier" by David Ferry. "The Soldier," with its clear, dramatic barracks scene, is characterized by Pinsky as attaining "a proselike openness of statement while incorporating and using a distinctly contemporary sense of the material world, its obdurate inhumanity and its human uses" (172). Ferry's poem, though quite different in its formal concerns from James Wright's poem, is a model of those qualities—restraint, clarity, and wholeness—that Wright himself pursued in his own work.

If we could combine the essence of Wright—what Pinsky describes as the "surrealist enterprise"—with Ferry's "proselike openness of statement," we would have a poem that points ahead to the dominant mode in American poetry from the late seventies until the present. That poem, a hybrid of sorts, was already being written by Simpson, Levine, and Dickey and would be taken up by seventies poets James Seay, Richard Tillinghast, Anne Stevenson, Clarence Major, and, to some extent, Ellen Bryant Voigt. Broadly speaking, this poem was a form of dramatic lyric that, depending on the poet, emphasized either the songlike quality of the lyric or the narrative movement and detail of story-drama. The immediate source of this dramatic lyric had come from the Academic poets and their precursors such as Ransom and Allen Tate. Although a lot of shifting and jostling had taken place in mainstream American poetry during the sixties, by the end of the seventies the center still found the qualities of control and reticence to be useful virtues. The lyricism that had been muffled by the intellectual and argumentative structures of the Academic style and had been declared conventional by many poets of the sixties began to return in poets such as Ellen Bryant Voigt. The opening stanza of Voigt's "Claiming Kin" is characteristic of the best and most rigorous of the new dramatic lyric:

> Insistent as a whistle, her voice up
> the stairs pried open the blanket's
> tight lid and piped me
> down to the pressure cooker's steam and rattle.
> In my mother's kitchen, the hot iron spit
>
> on signal, the vacuum cleaner whined
> and snuffled. Bright face
> and a snazzy apron, clicking her long spoons,
> how she commandeered the razzle-dazzle!

Perhaps what linked poets as diverse as James Wright and Ferry with those such as Ellen Bryant Voigt was the forceful presence of a governing tone or voice. In an essay published in the *American Poetry Review* in 1978, Stanley Plumly wrote, "Tone seems to have displaced the image as a 'technique of discovery'" (24). The shift in emphasis from a poetry governed by traditional prosody or by the minimalism of surrealist diction resulted, Plumly believed, in "a free verse more flexible than ever . . . to accommodate a wider, more detailed, even contradictory range of emotional experience—yes, accommodate and control" (24). Plumly had discovered in the American poetry of the seventies that as tone had become more intimate, more evocative of the voice and personality of the poet, the "territory of the poem became more detailed, discrete, named" (24). To say that tone and voice are the most significant aspects of American poetry since the mid-seventies simplifies the complexity and diversity of work written in the past twenty years. It also has the effect of broadening the definitions of those words until they become nearly meaningless or at best fuzzily associated with, as Ira Sadoff has pointed out, "tone of voice . . . mood," "point of view," and even "personality" (238). But it was not Plumly's intention to create a reductive description of mid-seventies American poetry; rather, tone and voice were ways to approach what Plumly saw as the increasingly formal characteristics of a ubiquitous free-verse "prose lyric" (27).

If Pinsky's ordering principle for American poetry in the mid-seventies was discursiveness—a wandering inside the materiality of the poem, in both its ideas and things—Plumly saw tone and voice as instruments that gave such wandering its control. Although Pinsky and Plumly recognized the power of the image as an icon or emblem, and the importance of the modernist inheritance the image represented, they both criticized Deep Imagism and surrealism for producing poems that were too reductive. Plumly summed up the overall frustration with the period style in this way: "The image alone has no voice" (25).

The development of the dramatic lyric as a common mode from the seventies until the present was also helped by the influence of confessional poetry. Confessional poetry created a kind of radical tradition of the self and offered an immediate and seemingly inexhaustible source of "voice"—the poet's own life.

James Wright, whose own poetry reflects the development of the contemporary dramatic lyric, remarked in a 1978 interview that "my own life is the only thing I have to begin with. It seems to me an aesthetically legitimate as well as a morally legitimate thing to try to figure out what one's own life really is" (176). The positioning of the self in the poem, depending on how it was handled, allowed poets to re-create, no matter how personal and intimate, any state of mind or human predicament. It is not an exaggeration to say that the dominant mode of American poetry, as reflected in the majority of Wesleyan poets published since the late seventies, has been a discursive, personal narrative, written in free verse that is tightly controlled by tone and voice. Even poets who have continued working in traditional forms subsumed convention to the overall atmosphere of tone and voice. Although American poets for more than a decade had invested heavily in Deep Imagism and surrealism, the period style had written itself out and had left poets searching for ways, through their personal experience, to write about the "obdurate inhumanity and . . . human uses" of the material world.

The permission that confessional poets granted young writers of the sixties and seventies was a permission to explore and create their own myths. These myths, though largely about the middle class and its suburban and mental landscapes, began to admit narrative shape and detail back into mainstream American poetry. The struggle by poets to define who they were not only as Americans but as individuals with unique voices was also part of the invitation implicit in the democratization of poetry by creative writing programs. This invitation became so powerful that, as Sadoff points out, "searching for a voice" is now a cliché of the creative writing workshops (238).

The Eighties and Nineties

As the Deep Image had done in the sixties and seventies, the prose lyric would come to dominate the poetry produced in creative writing workshops from the late seventies until the present. Unlike Deep Imagism, the terms of the "prose lyric" have always been broader. Wesleyan poets from the eighties working in this mode are as diverse as Garrett Hongo and Elizabeth Spires, Pattiann Rogers and Yusef Komunyakaa, Jordan Smith and Jane Hirshfield. The prose lyric possesses all the qualities of directness, sincerity, and honesty that had been the goal of many of the Wesleyan poets of the first decade. Garrett Hongo in "The Hongo Store" provides a powerful example of how the prose lyric produces a personal myth:

> My parents felt those rumblings
> Coming deep from the earth's belly,
> Thudding like the bell of the Buddhist Church.
> Tremors in the ground swayed the bathinette
> Where I lay squalling in soapy water.

And Elizabeth Spires in "Globe," with delicacy and exactitude, brings us back to one of her earliest memories:

> I spread my game on the cracked linoleum floor:
> I had to play inside all day.
> The woman who kept me said so.
> She was middle-aged, drank tea in the middle of the day,
> her face the color of dust layered on a table.

All prose lyrics have in common a surface realism of particular details which are used to establish a dramatic event in a specific time and place. The convention of time and place has created what Charles Altieri calls the "scenic" mode. Although the "scenic" mode characterizes many of the poets published by Wesleyan in the eighties and nineties, it is not the only period style represented.

Since the late seventies the poetry of John Ashbery has exerted a considerable influence on American poets. In part its evasions and ellipticisms, its iconography taken from popular culture, its playful use of cliché, its determination to subvert the old verities of love and beauty have provided an antidote to the "scenic" aspect of the prose lyric. As an antidote the Ashbery style has also been easily appropriated by creative writing workshops, resisting the emotive critical vocabulary of the workshop while allowing young poets to focus on the processes of language and to investigate the way in which consciousness and experience emerge through syntax. By the mid-eighties Ashbery had infiltrated mainstream American poetry enough to have established a signature mode in a younger generation of poets. Wesleyan poets Jane Miller, Olga Broumas, Ralph Angel, Bin Ramke, Donald Revell, and Brenda Hillman show the effect of Ashbery in their inventive work.

In the late seventies and early eighties, while the influence of the prose lyric and John Ashbery had established itself firmly in creative writing workshops, two movements—one reactionary and the other avant-garde—began developing on the fringes of mainstream American poetry. The reactionary movement has been loosely called New Formalism and is represented by poets and critics such as Dana Gioia, Brad Leithauser, and Joseph Epstein. The New Formalist aesthetic is characterized by a return to the conventions of the Academic poetry of the fifties. Brad Leithauser's essay "Metrical Illiteracy" criticized the tradition of American free verse for its formlessness, unmusicality, and self-involvement. The criticism in Leithauser's essay was mainly directed at those products of democracy, the poems written by poets trained in creative writing workshops. Another New Formalist critic, Robert McPhillips, believed that a renewed attention to form would allow "a significant number of younger poets to think and communicate clearly about their sense of what is of most human value—love, beauty, mortality" (207).

Lamenting the loss of American cultural coherence and purpose last felt in the fifties, New Formalism paralleled the conservative turn that had taken place in America during the seventies and eighties. New Formalism had little influence on the Wesleyan poets of the eighties. Jordan Smith, Sherod Santos, and Judith Baumel write elegant and formal poems which occasionally employ traditional conventions, but on the whole they are more interested in creating an intimate and direct voice, typical of the prose lyric, and in this way they oppose the "robust little music box," which Leithauser argued for in "Metrical Illiteracy."

Whereas New Formalism attempted to regain some of the aesthetic ground taken from it by the creative writing workshop prose lyric, an avant-garde movement that identified itself as Language poetry developed in opposition to everything that was not iconoclastic. Although in recent years, Language poetry, especially critical theory based on it, has become part of university creative writing and literature curricula, it has been primarily situated outside traditional cultural institutions. In fact Language poetry's main purpose is to criticize and deflate the coercive forces—political, social, and cultural—created by traditional institutions such as universities. As a result, Language poetry attempts to explore the ways in which traditional structures of language force poets to misrepresent the occasions of their experience. In many ways Language poetry contains the passion and energy that was found in the early Deep Image rhetoric of Robert Bly, yet it is closer to the technique-driven aesthetic of Olson's projective verse and therefore is suspicious of the powerful feeling and emotion Bly demanded that poetry embrace. The influence of Language poetry on the Wesleyan poets of the eighties and nineties has been very slight, and yet in the work of Susan Howe, Donald Revell, and Walid Bitar a reader encounters some of its concerns.

The Wesleyan Tradition is not meant to predict in any specific way the trends and movements that might arise in the next ten or twenty years in American poetry. Rather it offers a way in which to assess the Wesleyan University Press poetry program's original and ongoing function—to publish what in the broadest terms was truly the best in American poetry. In doing this the program has helped to define and develop a poetry that is clearly American, one that is both popular and serious, that defines, criticizes, and supports the democratic institutions of American culture, and that in four decades has come to represent the cultural pluralism of democracy anticipated by Tocqueville more than 150 years ago.

Postscript

Fifteen years have passed since I compiled *The Wesleyan Tradition* and in that time the Wesleyan poetry program has continued to flourish. If in the fifties the program was a place where the Academic mainstream found one of its most vivid expressions, in the past fifteen years, it has become a place where avant-garde and Language poetries, having been conventionalized into the cultural mainstream by creative writing programs, have found a reliable home. Poets such as Joan Rettalack, Leslie Scalapino, Barbara Guest, and Rae Armantrout who once relied almost solely on small presses to publish their work now have a supportive and committed publisher and a centralized system for distribution. Since irony is a major feature of modernism, it is not surprising that these poets who had once created much of their identity by fiercely contrasting themselves with Academic or university-based poets are now securely a part of the new cultural imperium, but this, of course, is a familiar story of cultural tectonics.

WORKS CITED

Altieri, Charles. *Self and Sensibility in Contemporary American Poetry.* Cambridge University Press, 1984.

Bly, Robert. "Looking for Dragon Smoke." In *Naked Poetry,* ed. Stephen Berg and Robert Mezey. Bobbs Merrill, 1969.

———. "The Words of Robert Creeley." *The Fifties,* vol. 2. 1959. Reprint by Hobart and William Smith College Press in association with *The Seneca Review.*

———. "A Wrong Turning in American Poetry." Reprinted in *Claims for Poetry,* ed. Donald Hall. University of Michigan Press, 1984.

Dickey, James. "Louis Simpson." In *Babel to Byzantium.* Farrar, Straus and Giroux, 1968. Also reprinted in *On Louis Simpson,* ed. Hank Lazer (University of Michigan Press, 1968).

Epstein, Joseph. "Who Killed Poetry?" *Commentary* 86 (August 1988).

Gioia, Dana. *Can Poetry Matter? Essays on Poetry and American Culture.* Graywolf Press, 1992.

Leithauser, Brad. "Metrical Illiteracy." *New Criterion* 1, no. 5 (1983).

Levine, Philip. "Mine Own John Berryman." *Gettysburg Review* 4, no. 4 (1991).

McPhillips, Robert. "What's New about New Formalism." In *Expansive Poetry.* Storyline Press, 1989.

Pearson, Norman Holmes. *Decade: A Collection of Poetry from the First Ten Years of the Wesleyan Poetry Program.* Wesleyan University Press, 1969.

Pinsky, Robert. *The Situation of Poetry.* Princeton University Press, 1976.

Plumly, Stanley. "Chapter and Verse." *American Poetry Review* (January–February 1978).

Sadoff, Ira. "Hearing Voices: The Fiction of Poetic Voice." In *An Ira Sadoff Reader: Selected Prose and Poetry.* University Press of New England, 1993.

Tocqueville, Alexis de. *Democracy in America.* Schocken, 1961.

Von Hallberg, Robert. *American Poetry and Culture, 1945–1980.* Harvard University Press, 1985.

Wallace, Ronald. *Vital Signs: Contemporary American Poetry from the University Presses.* University of Wisconsin Press, 1989.

Wright, James. "The Delicacy of Walt Whitman." In *Collected Prose.* University of Michigan Press, 1983.

———. "Poetry Must Think." In *Collected Prose.* University of Michigan Press, 1983.

Zweig, Paul. "American Poetry Restored. Review of A Revolution in Taste." *New York Times,* December 17, 1978. Reprinted in *On Louis Simpson,* ed. Hank Lazer (University of Michigan Press, 1988).

———. "The New Surrealism." In *Contemporary Poetry in America,* ed. Robert Boyers. Schocken, 1974.

III

An Interview by Matt Barry

ON A BRISK AND BLUE DAY I met Michael Collier. I was in Virginia for a week of business and on Saturday morning drove from Richmond to Maryland through a simply stunning countryside. From the moment I stepped through Michael and Katherine's front door I felt that I was in a welcoming and serene home. After some time Michael and I went out the kitchen door, crunched our way over to the outdoor stairs leading to his office over the garage, and promptly settled in. A conversation began that spanned into the late afternoon. When I awoke the next morning—to the inviting smell of bacon, eggs, and coffee—my hosts had already gone for their swim.

In the following interview, Michael Collier eloquently invites us into some of the memorable and impressionable moments in his life that shaped him as a writer and motivated him to dedicate his life to his writing and teaching. The thoughts he shares in this interview are especially valuable for readers who are grappling with decisions that will impact their life paths in monumental ways. Collier's resolve to become a writer demonstrates to us as students, artists, or truth-seekers that the seemingly insurmountable struggles to uncover our own "calling" require little more, and never less, than pure determination and discipline to overcome. His penetrating curiosity, sparkling wit, and quiet humility coalesce into a fine portrait of poetry in America today.

The purpose of the On Poetry interview series is to provide a space for us to hear from a variety of highly accomplished and seasoned voices. Voices who can help us better understand, not only their work, but also how we can make a connection back to our own craft. In the end, so that we may better understand how to use our own talents to create lives rich with art.

The Grove Review: Well, I'm sitting here with Michael Collier in what you might call his writing studio. Is that what you would call this?
Michael Collier: Yeah, that's what I would call this, or my office.

TGR: Your office. And we're in Catonsville, Maryland.
MC: Yes. The site of the Catonsville Nine.

TGR: While I want to ask you about many things, I'd like to start out with your childhood and educational experiences. Would you mind starting there?
MC: Sure. I was born in Phoenix, Arizona, in 1953 and grew up there. My father had moved from the Midwest after the Second World War. When he first arrived he sold mattresses. He was part of that mid-twentieth-century westward movement. Phoenix was a small city at that time. Growing up there I had the sense that I lived in the middle of nowhere—a strange, hot, and inhospitable environment. I didn't find it congenial, even from early on. I went to parochial schools in Phoenix—I was taught by nuns from the Institute of the Blessed Virgin Mary, and then in high school by Jesuits.

My education wasn't unique, but to me it was interesting. The nuns were wonderful and strange, like aliens, driven by a zealous and conservative Roman Catholicism. They liked to scare the crap out of us with stories about what happened to sinful boys and girls. The bloody crucifixes in each classroom, the cat-o-nine tails affect of the rosaries they wore around their waists, the wimples, the thickly padded habits and skirts were all House of Horrors stuff. They were good at corporal punishment. They terrified me but they also turned me into a nimble skeptic.

TGR: Do you carry some of those stories with you still?

MC: Oh, yeah. It completely influences the way I see the world. I'm drawn at times to writing about the violence inherent in human relationships, and I have to think this is connected to the sadistic and gothic stories the nuns spun in order to keep us in line. One nun in particular, Mother Myron, elicited praise for herself from us by rapping a wooden door stop on the edge of our desks at the end of each school day. As she did this she said, "Treating you." It was meant to be a question: How am I treating you? But it sounded like a command. She didn't want us to say, "You're treating us terribly," which was the truth. We had to say, each of us, "Fine, Mother." Deviation from the script wasn't permitted. You have someone banging a wooden doorstop on your desk like that each day of the fourth grade and it stays with you. God bless her. She lived longer than the prophets and had shrunk so much before she died she was barely larger than her shoes. The nuns provided me with my first encounter with Negative Capability.

In the sixth, seventh, and eighth grades, and on into high school I was a Knight of the Altar, an altar boy—until I was eighteen! This was at the beginning of Vatican II, and I had to learn the Latin Mass as well as the newer, idiom-friendly vernacular Mass. I loved the ceremony and ritual and music of the liturgy. The rhythm and cadence of the language . . . and the patterns of the prayers and responses were transporting and mysterious. I remember feeling in church that this was all incredibly beautiful.

TGR: You talked about the nuns and the aesthetic that you may have carried forward in some of your pieces—violence as an underlying theme in your work, for example. Are there general connections between your childhood awakenings, or do you now look back and see specific experiences that had a very specific influence on your writing?

MC: I don't know exactly because I think that we're mostly aware of these awakenings in retrospect. But your question about influences reminds me of the importance that singing had on me.

I enjoyed singing in church or in the classroom, which we did frequently. Not only did the sound of our voices sound beautiful but it could often seem as if I was losing myself in the larger group, disappearing into the music we made with our voices. I believe that singing helped tune my ear and developed a receptiveness to language in me.

Encountering the Jesuits was profoundly important and influential as well. It might have been the first day of high school that my theology teacher said, "Now the first thing I want you to do, everybody, is to forget *everything* the nuns taught you." And so, what that did was to validate the skepticism I had always felt about the strange, sometimes loving, but mostly threatening and punishing nuns. The Jesuits demanded that we doubt, test, and question our beliefs, our faith in God.

For a while I thought seriously about becoming a priest. In grade school, on Vocation Day, priests would come to talk to the boys about entering the seminary and the nuns would speak to the girls about entering the convent. A vocation was a calling, they would tell us. God called you to the priesthood. That's why it was important to listen to God, so you wouldn't miss hearing him and the higher purpose he had for you. The idea that you came to an understanding of your purpose in life by listening to a voice that was both inside and outside of you was appealing to me because it was so mysterious. In high school when I saw how the Jesuits lived, profoundly engaged with the world, profoundly intellectual and spiritual, I found myself attracted to a way of life—never mind that it was in the service of Jesus Christ—that was both spiritual and intellectual. I broached the idea of joining the Jesuits, when I was a senior, with one of the teachers that influenced me greatly. In fact, he's one of the people to whom *The Ledge* is dedicated, Michael Moynahan. I confessed this fledgling desire to him in a letter. His response was generous for what it did not try to do, which was to encourage me. He was happy for me, but I suppose he was fatalistic about my ever entering the Order. And then the fever passed.

TGR: And that was it? Your passion for that path came and went?

MC: Yeah. I found poetry. I found literature. And as I began to read more poetry and poets I saw that poetry was also a calling or vocation. There was certainly nothing in my family or background that suggested poetry and literature could be a substitute for religion. In high school I was mostly a jock. And yet I began to cultivate this completely other life, an inner life. Although as a kid I read books. My mother told me that reading was the most important thing you could do, and for some reason, even though I rarely saw her read—she didn't have the time—I believed her.

TGR: How young were you when you remember reading in earnest?

MC: In the summers, there was nothing to do in the afternoon. It was too blistering hot to go outside. So I read books. I read all of the Hornblower books by C. S. Forester one summer, and the next all of the Oz books. One thing I liked about reading was how it transported you to another world and allowed you to live inside of it. I also liked the feeling of accomplishment it provided, especially when I would tear through a multivolume work. There was a simple acquisitive pleasure from gauging the number of pages I'd read in a day or an hour.

There was, and still is, a materialistic aspect to the reading process that spurred me on to compete with myself. Most of my reading was done during the summer. During the school year, I didn't read much. In eighth grade I was in charge of the Scholastic Book Club, which meant if I could get my class as a whole to buy, let's say, six books, then I got one free.

TGR: That was the motivation?

MC: Yeah [*laughs*]. A bit pathetic, I admit. And then later in high school I realized that I didn't want to play football anymore. I hated it as well as the coaches, the practices, the mentality you had to adopt. It was clear to me I wasn't going to get as big as I'd need to be to save myself from getting stomped on the field. So I gave that up. I probably needed another identity, one that would integrate with the inklings of an inner life I was beginning to feel. I put all of my efforts into my studies and reading. Outside reading was a part of studying as far as I was concerned.

TGR: How many brothers and sisters do you have?

MC: I have four sisters. I have a younger sister. So I'm the fourth. My father was a Big Ten Conference champion sprinter at Indiana University at the same time Jesse Owens competed for Ohio State. The room I slept in doubled as my father's office. On the wall were pictures of him with Jesse Owens and other well-known trackmen of the time. When I woke in the morning or turned the light out before I went to bed, the first and last thing I saw was my father as an athletic young man, standing next to other athletes, one of whom was legendary. Because I was so familiar with these photographs, it's hard to say what their specific inspiration was but they did inspire me. Although my father was a quiet and humble man, these pictures spoke for themselves and the achievements they represented.

My sister, Jeanne, who is seven years older than me, competed in the 1964 Summer Olympics in Tokyo, where she won a silver medal in springboard diving. Her accomplishment had a potent effect on my family. My father was able to live out a dream for himself because he had never made it to the Olympics, and the buoyancy he got from her triumph was palpable. To me, a sixth grader, I enjoyed being in the shadow of her success. I was also aware that her success hadn't come easily. Her daily example of what it meant to practice and improve and excel at something made a lasting impression on me. Also, I understand now that there is a relationship between what she did as a diver—making beautiful figures with her body in the air—and what I would like to do with words and language, as a poet. I'm grateful for her example and grateful too for my father's more quiet and distant example.

TGR: High expectations just by example.

MC: By example, yes.

TGR: And did that lead to discipline for you?

MC: Maybe for me it did.

TGR: What fascinates me about that is the knowledge that while there are a lot of bright people in the world, only a very few are able to do what you are doing. Beyond the talent, the raw ingredients, there is the required dedication or discipline to put one foot in front of the other to keep going. Listening to you, I wonder how having those examples of achievement played into your motivation to succeed?

MC: Yeah, I think that's possible. I have to tell you that we weren't a distinguished family in terms of the Phoenix, Arizona, establishment. We were completely middle class. My father was a traveling salesman. But there was a prevailing sense that you could do and should do something with your life.

TGR: Anything else in the category of early influences, whether you can think of specific people, specific teachers, specific books, or experiences that you have, that you haven't already shared?

MC: I learn best from direct contact with other people and, luckily, all along there were people who influenced me. I suppose I've always needed to be part of a group of some kind. Perhaps because growing up in Arizona I saw myself as isolated. We made snowmen by stacking up tumbleweeds and spraying them with some kind of white gloppy stuff that passed for snow. One of the neighbors I grew up with was an elderly gentleman, a chemist, who lived across the street. Almost every evening, along with other kids, I would go with him to walk his dogs. He was a substitute grandfather, but he also had a talent for treating us seriously. He stressed the importance of school, told us to take Latin, and in general to be curious about the world. I don't know how he did it, perhaps it was in his nature or temperament, but he made the future look interesting and hopeful. Somehow his own curiosity was planted in us. By the way, he was a very good amateur magician, which was part of his charm.

TGR: He would engage you?

MC: He would engage you, yeah. And treat you at a level a little bit higher than your parents would. One time he told me, "It's very important not to join a group, or lose yourself in a group." And that kind of ran counter to my membership in church, the Boy Scouts, and the football team, and my desire to defuse the isolation I experienced living in the wastes of the Southwest. He was probably the only person on the block who didn't go to church. But every Sunday he visited St. Joseph's Hospital, bringing magazines to the sick and performing magic for the ill children. There was more than a measure of quiet integrity in him. And now that I think of it, he looked like William Carlos Williams.

TGR: After high school, what were your subsequent educational experiences?

MC: After high school I ended up at Santa Clara University, in California, mostly because it's a Jesuit school.

TGR: What year did you attend?

MC: I was there in 1971–72. The day I arrived I realized I would have to transfer to some other school. Santa Clara was merely a larger version of the Jesuit high school I'd just graduated from, except it was coed.

TGR: You were eighteen then?

MC: Yes, I was eighteen. That summer I had started to write in earnest, spurred on by an electric typewriter my mother had given me for graduation. One of her brothers worked for Royal Typewriter. It was a basic model and the keys were always jamming. Everyday I would put a piece of paper in the roller and fill it up with words. It wasn't poetry I was writing—I don't know what it was. Prose of a kind, I guess.

TGR: Was it narrative?

MC: Yeah, it was mainly narrative, but very impressionistic and overwrought in its imagery and emotion and overloaded with adjectives and abstractions. It was something I felt compelled to do. Language rushed out of me and it was all I could do to get it down. It was a bitch when those keys jammed and the sublime torrent was stymied! It was completely unrevisable, even if I had known what revision was. Writing a page a day taught me something about the habit of writing, and the accountant in me liked the fact that at the end of three months I had almost a hundred pages. And that summer I read a tremendous amount. I life-guarded at a pool at a condominium where, basically, I sat under an umbrella and read books all day.

TGR: And got paid.
MC: And got paid. [*laughs*] And no one ever complained. Occasionally I would look up to see if everybody was okay. But I read three or four or more books a week. And then I would write, and hang out with my buddies. When I went to Santa Clara I was already feeling restless. I wanted to be a writer, but I didn't know what that meant. At one point when I had finished a book, I thought how amazing it would be to put that many words together. But I felt as if I couldn't. I felt that it was beyond my ability ever to be able to do that. But it loomed as a kind of challenge, as an enticement, as a goal. When I got to Santa Clara, the scene wasn't very interesting to me. I wanted to be in another part of the country. I wanted to be with different people. So I plotted an escape almost the moment I arrived. I switched majors from political science to English. And then I thought if I could get my parents to agree to let me study in Europe, I would go to England. It turned out it was an easy sell because a semester in England was much cheaper than a semester at Santa Clara. We worked out a deal where I would go to school in London for a semester, travel for a bit, and then return home and find a job. During this time I would have applied to other schools to transfer. I wanted to go east to a college or university that had an established writer on its faculty.

I had read in a review of a John Updike novel in *Time* that Updike's mother had looked at an anthology of American poetry and had noticed most of the famous contributors in the anthology had gone to Harvard. And that's how John Updike ended up at Harvard. So very naively I thought, *OK, I need to go to Harvard, and if that doesn't work out, a school where there's a writer.* I applied to Harvard, Yale, Amherst, and some other place. I'd been a good student in high school, but I didn't have a chance at getting into these schools. I had none of the wherewithal or sophistication that those students possessed. And then I also applied to Connecticut College because I had been reading the poems of William Meredith, and noticed that he taught there. Before I went to England, I flew to New York, put all of my luggage in two coin lockers, and hitchhiked out of JFK, through New England, visiting schools for two weeks. The uncle who worked for Royal Typewriter lived near Boston. I stayed with him for a few days, a nice bit of synchronicity.

TGR: So during this time you're coming up with your master plan.

MC: Yes, I was coming up with my master plan. I went to a number of schools and was deciding whether or not to visit Connecticut College when my aunt serendipitously suggested, "You know, you should look at Connecticut College, because they just started to let men in." It used to be a women's college. It ended up being the only place I was accepted, eager as it was to admit men. My notion to go study with a writer and the way I went about it was naive, but the instinct was accurate.

TGR: Pretty good instinct.

MC: Perhaps, but it could have been disastrous. I was fortunate that William Meredith recognized what I was about from the early going. And because of his astute generosity, he knew how to channel my energy and ambition. He just took me on as a challenge and we're still very close today. I finished my studies at Connecticut College in December 1975, and graduated with the class of '76.

TGR: That's pretty driven for an eighteen- or nineteen-year-old.

MC: I admit, I was very driven.

TGR: That's not a typical eighteen- or nineteen-year-old's response to that time of life. I mean, study abroad? Okay. But showing up someplace and deciding right off that this isn't going to work, and then going right back through the application process, that seems pretty motivated.

MC: That's why I mentioned earlier that the notion of a vocation was so important. I felt I was being called to write. The great thing about wanting to do anything in the arts is that if you show the least interest and diligence, often there's someone to encourage you. Someone's going to push you because it rekindles their passion for what they do as well. I was plain lucky in throwing myself at William Meredith. I don't think he'd ever had anybody simply show up and say, "Here I am! This is what I'm about."

TGR: Do you remember that encounter well?

MC: Oh yeah. It's absolutely vivid. I showed up in New London at the end of August, during the 1972 Munich Olympics, on an incredibly hot and humid day. I had been hitchhiking and when I got to the college, I went into the biggest building, found a bathroom, shrugged myself out of my T-shirt, and changed into a button-down shirt and corduroy sports coat crammed in the bottom of my pack. At the admissions office I spoke with Jane Bredeson, an admissions officer, who, once she found out my interests, sent me over to the English department in Thames Hall. She had just seen "Bill" heading in that direction. I was coming up the cramped back staircase of rickety Thames Hall at the same time Meredith was going down, carrying a heavy standard typewriter. The air was steamy and thick. I announced my intentions and after a moment's pause, he asked me to come back up to his office to talk, but before that he needed to put the typewriter in his car. In his office I told him that I'd read his poems, and that I was interested in applying. He heard me out and said my plan sounded good, and to keep him informed. We talked about Robert Lowell and John Berryman. John Berryman, especially, was someone I had been reading heavily, and I had noticed that Berryman had dedicated more of the *Dream Songs* to Meredith than anyone else. I asked him—and I recognize this moment now so well because it happens to me occasionally—I said, "Would you mind if I sent you a few of my poems?" And there was a kind of pause, and then he said, "Certainly, but I'm not a very good correspondent." I did send him some poems, but I never heard from him.

A year later I presented myself at the start of the school year. I can't say for sure he remembered me. Maybe he did. I think he did, but it wasn't, "Oh yeah! Welcome! Let's get down to business." I had to prove myself and win him over first. He saw I was serious. And he tried to meet that seriousness. He was generous about including me in not only the literary life of the college but his own life as well. When Robert Lowell gave a reading in Cambridge in 1974, Meredith asked me to go along with him. After the reading, Lowell invited Meredith to a party at Frank Bidart's apartment and I tagged along. At the party everyone got to sit beside Lowell, as if having an audience with the pope, for a few minutes. This wasn't orchestrated in any way. It was part of the social flow of the evening and Lowell's own desire to engage with people. There were many other times that Meredith included me in gatherings like this and they became part of my education.

TGR: You talked for a bit about becoming a person who writes poetry. You've read a great deal and you started writing fairly early on. When did you realize you were being drawn specifically to poetry versus something else?

MC: When I first started to write, earlier than the summer of filling up pages, I was trying to write poems. But the source of those poems was an inchoate need to express emotions. When I'm giving a reading at a public library, sometimes I'll ask the audience to raise their hands if they write poems. A few people are apt to respond. And then I'll ask, "How many of you have ever written a poem?" A few more people raise their hands. And then I almost always say, "And the rest of you are liars." Liars, because I think that almost everybody has tried to use language to express the powerful feelings they've had and the form this writing most often takes is poetry. Like most people, I tried writing poems before I had read much poetry, so my models were songwriters like Simon and Garfunkel or Bob Dylan. Other than the hymns I'd learned at school and church, or the patterns made by liturgical language, popular songs were as close to poetry as I had come. Popular songs are actually good training wheels for poetry because so many of them are based on the ballad.

TGR: You've named some poets who were influences. Can you think of others earlier on that had an impact on you?

MC: When I was a senior in high school I read the metaphysical poets. John Donne's *Holy Sonnets* appealed to me because they contained a violence of language and an eroticized spirituality. I didn't know what the poems were saying but I responded to the rhythm and sounds of the words. A little bit of Wordsworth made sense to me, like *Tintern Abbey*. *Tintern Abbey* made sense. But Keats didn't. Keats didn't appeal to me. I wouldn't have known to call it this at the time, but Keats felt precious.

TGR: Too much?

MC: Yeah. Too rich for my unsophisticated taste. On the other hand, poets that my friends were reading avidly in high school, like Ferlinghetti and Ginsberg, didn't appeal to me in the least. The Beats seemed fraudulent. Perhaps I considered them fraudulent because some of the students who advocated them struck poses I didn't care for. They were the hippies of the school, although hippies at a Jesuit school had to follow the dress and tonsorial code like everyone else; they were low-carb hippies. I was still in "jock land." I would read Ginsberg and I would think, well, it's cool, it's sort of cool, but I just didn't get it.

The other poets I began to read in the summer before I went to college were Sylvia Plath and Dylan Thomas. I found *Ariel* because it was one of the few poetry books you could buy in the mall bookstores. With Plath and Dylan Thomas I liked to walk around the living room when I was alone and read the poems aloud. Again, I understood very little of the poems but I enjoyed forming the words and hearing them and most importantly feeling, the resonance, the vibrations, they made inside my body.

But it probably wasn't until the middle of my freshman year in college that I began to make significant distinctions between poets. I have always been drawn to more formal poets like Robert Frost over William Carlos Williams. It took me a long time to come to William Carlos Williams. And then, working with William Meredith, I was influenced by some of his formal preoccupations. After I graduated from Connecticut College, especially in graduate school, I had to undo some of what I learned as a matter of opening up. Other poets who were early influences included Anthony Hecht and early Robert Lowell, which, at the time, I preferred to late Lowell—and W. H. Auden, Philip Larkin.

TGR: It seems like early on you already had some pretty firm sensibilities.

MC: Well, I think sensibility is aligned with temperament. Where does temperament come from? I'm not exactly sure, but I did find myself taking sides almost reflexively. I much prefer looking at a beautiful still life than I do abstract expressionism. And you'll find people who can't stand to look at a still life become completely engrossed in abstract expressionism. This preference doesn't mean I don't admire abstraction, and take a lot of pleasure from it. But in a room of paintings I would be drawn to a Vermeer or a Brueghel because I'm interested in all the human life represented on the canvas. And not so interested in the kind of larger emotional, or even impressionistic impulses that abstraction generates. And why that is, I don't know. It just is.

TGR: I suppose you just do or you don't. This is a nice bridge to the notion of voice. What does that mean to you, and how did you come to develop or define your own over time?

MC: Voice is a very squishy subject. Generally, we believe that voice develops, that it's a product of maturation, but we also believe that it involves listening to something inside of us that's unique. It's also supposed to have the quality of a signature and we don't quite know what it is until we see or hear it. Voice contains tone and mood. In other words, it comprises an atmosphere.

The mystery is how we acquire one and how we perpetuate it. On Robert Frost's last trip to the West Coast, in the early sixties, he invited William Meredith to accompany him. At some point, he and Frost got into an argument and when it was over Frost said, "I brought you along so you could see how I take myself." Perhaps voice is the poem's way of registering how we take ourselves.

TGR: And can be identified uniquely with you?
MC: Yes. I don't know if I've answered your question about voice. I don't know what my voice as a poet sounds like. I suspect if I could hear it I'd have the same unsettled feeling I have when I hear a recording of my voice. "Is that what I sound like?" Maybe the closest we get to knowing our own voice is by hearing it in other poets' work. For me, I strongly identify with Philip Larkin, Thomas Hardy, Randall Jarrell, and George Herbert. Sometimes I'll write a line and think to myself, "Oh, that's Hardy, or Jarrell." It's not likely that any one else would hear or see the connection.

TGR: Is it in the language or is it in an implied worldview?
MC: I think it's very hard to separate the two because how one looks at the world in larger terms is so wedded to the language one uses to express it. We begin to locate our voice by echo-locating with other poets. Meredith was heavily influenced by Auden and worried that people would find him out. He pointed a few passages out to me, and of course they sounded nothing like Auden, but he was self-conscious because he could see a connection even if no one else could. As inveterate plagiarists we stand naked before our masters, but it is from this exposure that we discover our voices.

TGR: Is part of that humility or a sense of anxiety caused by a self-inflicted doubt, a question of whether you are truly innovating in the sense of this huge tradition? Is the question whether you are really doing something new and different, versus derivative?
MC: No, I don't think so. Wrestling with your influences, trying to differentiate yourself from your influences is a different

process than the anxiety about being derivative. Innovation comes about by absorbing convention or tradition of a particular kind. And that happens on two levels. I have in mind Eliot's notion that there are the artists who create, who do the original work, the revolutionaries. And there are those who refine and refine. They both play important roles in the tradition of poetry. I think even those originators who you might often think of as being rebellious or iconoclastic absorbed various traditions. Ginsberg is a good example of this. *Howl,* when it was published, was considered fresh and startling and provocative, yet it is beholden to the *King James Bible,* Blake, Christopher Smart, Whitman, and others. And yet, to use a very contemporary term, the "buzz" around it hyped its originality. It's anything but. There's a sourcebook about *Howl.* And it includes a holographic copy of an early draft of *Howl* along with letters, reviews, and notes about the poem. Do you know this book? It's one of my favorites.

TGR: No, I don't. I'll have to look it up.
MC: Oh, it's fantastic. In one of the appendices Ginsberg lists the influences in the poem. They're very specific. Shelley. Blake. It's very interesting. Some of what Ginsberg says about *Howl* is the result of hindsight and there's a self-consciousness to it. I guess what I want to say is that originality has its debts to pay and these debts are what create the threads that run through literary and artistic traditions.

TGR: There are deeper echoes.
MC: Yeah. And the tradition is somehow absorbed and transformed into something that feels more immediate and new.

TGR: Can Pound's work be thought of in this way?
MC: I think Pound is the kind of poet Eliot had in mind when he thought of an innovator. Pound stirred the pot. Although his poems aren't much quoted—lines here or there from the *Cantos,* "Hang it all, Robert Browning, / There can be but the one Sordello"—or maybe something that's epigrammatic, "The object is always the adequate symbol." But what he did was set a course for

many of the major developments in twentieth-century poetry. Not just in American poetry, but really all around the world. His genius was in his ability to synthesize and recognize connections between different cultures and genres. But this shouldn't be taken for refining a tradition. Pound wanted to enlarge poetry until it burst. Compared to Eliot's *Four Quartets,* the *Cantos* aren't usually thought of as having been successful. But their effect on poetry ultimately has been greater than Eliot's.

TGR: Moving more directly to your poems, can you talk a bit about the different structural elements of your work? What jumps out in your mind when you think about discussing your work?

MC: What jumps out at me now is how hard it is to write a poem. It used to seem a little easier, but it has gotten more difficult. Quite often I'll work in regular stanzas, quatrains, tercets, and sometimes five-line stanzas, and occasionally a little bit longer. I try to keep the syllable count balanced from line to line and, generally, I'll pay attention to the play of the iambic foot. This way I can keep the work as musical as possible but also loose so that the tone is never far from the colloquial. Those are the main things I have in mind. Actually, it's hard to say I have them in mind because the main element I pay attention to is the rhythm of the line, and once I get that down other things begin to fall in place. If I don't have a bit of music—a line that feels rhythmical—then I can't write the poem. Syntax is important as well. I like to develop long sentences with a lot of subordination. Syntax is the score over which the melody, so to speak, is played. And the stanza is more like the regulating device for the syntax, parceling it out and creating dramatic emphasis.

TGR: The passages.
MC: Yes. It offers a resistance against the colloquial or idiomatic aspect of the language.

TGR: You say you always start with music?
MC: I always start with music.

TGR: How does that happen?

MC: It's usually a single word or a phrase.

TGR: And does this word or phrase come to you in the present moment, or is it something you may have captured before?

MC: It's usually connected to an event, or I'm reading something, or it's triggered by a memory.

TGR: Do you do most of your writing here?

MC: Yeah.

TGR: And you're somewhere else and you see something that triggers.

MC: It doesn't happen. Rarely.

TGR: Then you don't carry a journal around with you?

MC: I don't carry a journal. There were times when I did, but now I don't. Because I found that if I wrote something down and then I tried to go back to it, I had a difficult time re-creating the moment. I'd gone deaf to it. It's very rare that while walking around I'm struck by an idea for a poem or I hear its initiating music. In fact, it's better if I don't. If it feels like I'm being brought to the edge of a poem, I resist thinking about it. If I try to pursue and develop it there and then, I usually destroy the delicacy of the moment. I've learned to sit at my desk and let my imagination find the experiences necessary for making a poem.

TGR: Structurally, how does that happen for you every day?

MC: It really depends. What's interesting about doing anything for a long time is that it's constantly changing, and what forces it to change are external circumstances. Right now, really for the last five years, or even longer, especially since I started directing the Bread Loaf Writers' Conference, I don't have as much time or the same kind of time I used to have. And even when I do have time, I find that I'm more easily distracted. I write for much shorter periods now—an hour or half hour, occasionally two hours. And in terms of my anxiety about writing, well, I'm as anxious as ever. But there's never been a time in my life when I thought I was writing enough. The output is parsimonious.

TGR: You mentioned a half hour to an hour. Is that a typical daily experience, a handful of days a week?

MC: Yes, I would say a handful of days. I take what I can get. I'm going to be away from home next week. I won't write at all. It's hard coming back and starting back up again. The writing process for me is much more fragmented now. It used to define my day in a much different way, much more completely. But these things evolve. I'm curious to see what the future will bring.

TGR: Can you walk me through a little bit more of the process itself? How do you choose an entry point? When do you know a poem is finished? What is your refining or revising process? What does that all look like for you?

MC: It's long and it's painstaking. In almost every other aspect of my life I'm impatient. I like to get things done. However, in writing poems apparently I have unlimited patience because I'm never worried about trying to finish a poem on any sort of schedule. I accept, and always have accepted, the fact that a poem will get finished at some point. So there are poems that I'll work on for many, many years. Not every year, not every day, but I'll keep them around and go back to them to see if I have a way of bringing it a little further along the path. This happened with a poem in *The Ledge,* "Argos." I started "Argos" in 1983 and I completed it in, I think, 1998. I knew I would finish it some decade [*laughs*].

TGR: That was some journey.

MC: It was a journey. What was peculiar about that poem, and I didn't know it until I finished it, was that I hadn't lived long enough. I didn't have enough experience to know what that poem was leading me to or "what it was about," and I just had to live longer to figure it out. A year or two would go by and I wouldn't futz with it. But it was one of the poems that I went back to again and again and again. I just thought the beginning was too solid to give up on. When I did finally figure out how to finish it I was grateful that it took so long because I learned much more about the peculiarities of the writing process by letting it hang fire. Over the years I had written several endings for the poem but they were false.

TGR: How did you know it was truly done after that much time?
MC: The poem is about Ulysses's return to Ithaca and his coming upon Argos, the dog he'd left behind twenty years before. It took me fifteen years of working on the poem to realize that I was writing about my own absence from my birthplace, and that if I were to return I would be a stranger not only to everyone else but also to myself. I couldn't have known that when I started writing the poem in 1983, but that is what I was led to.

TGR: That's a wonderful story. Can you talk a bit about teaching and the relationship between teaching and writing for you?
MC: I think, like other things, it changes. When I first started to teach I was teaching myself as much as I was teaching the students. I was learning how to talk about literature. I was learning how to spot things in poems that would be helpful for me as well as for my students. In some ways I was my own student. And it didn't feel like anything separate from writing. It felt like the necessary adjunct to writing. Where else in the culture do you really get to talk about what you love except in a classroom?

After having taught at the University of Maryland for more than twenty years, I find that what I'm doing now is imparting, or making available, a set of particular responses to art and literature. I don't learn so much directly from teaching any longer, the way I used to learn, though I learn plenty from the students, through their openness and passion. But what I do learn is a constant reminder from students about how necessary it is to keep open to the world and experience. And that's very important. I remind myself that teaching is a good thing to be doing because it's necessary and it still feels complementary with my life as a poet.

TGR: Back to the process of writing. Can you talk about what happens physically when you're in your study here?

MC: There's a lot of staring down at the page. There's a good deal of fidgeting. Quite often I'll start reading something. It might be a new book of poems that has come my way, or I'll feel disaffected from everything new and I'll go back and read something that I haven't read in a long time—Thomas Hardy, George Herbert, or Andrew Marvell. You know, a touchstone poet for me. Sometimes, I'll use Robert Frost as a way of figuring out how to create an argument in a poem I'm trying to write. There's a lot of getting up and walking around and looking at other things and trying really hard to distract myself. The hope is that at some point I either start writing something new, putting some new words down, or I find a way into an old poem. More and more, what happens is I'm working sort of like an accountant. I go back over poems again and again and again that aren't quite finished, looking for ways to open them up and create something strange and interesting. There's a lot of time looking at drafts of poems. I'm fairly indiscriminate about this activity. I don't have the drafts ordered in any kind of hierarchy. They're all mixed together no matter what phase of incompletion they might occupy.

TGR: And you're typing all these out?

MC: It depends. When I'm going through my folder, the boneyard, quite often what I'll do is start working in the margins of a page, noodling with a pen or pencil. This doesn't put much pressure on me, very little commitment, so I'm more apt to fake myself into writing something useful. Then, if I've gotten a couple lines and am lucky enough to create an opening, I'll put a sheet of paper in the typewriter and retype the entire draft. The physical activity of typing the poem authenticates the process for me in a way that writing by hand doesn't. I don't think that one method is better than the other. W. H. Auden declared that the typewriter would be the ruination of writing. For him, writing with a pen was a tactile and expressive gesture. The typewriter was a machine and stood between him and the uniqueness of his hand.

TGR: Let me take you back to the comment you made about working to try and open up a piece a bit more. What is happening when you work on that? And do you go through some sort of algorithm of things you're looking to tweak, or is the process more organic?

MC: No, it's more like waiting for a moment of inspiration. Often we think of inspiration as being the initiatory or originating impulse. For me, inspiration, or intuition, often occurs midway or near the end of working on a poem. So, in early drafts I try to get as much of that initial impulse down as possible, and then when I go back, I try to find ways of making the impulse strange or interesting. I'm patient enough, I think, to wait for an insight that I hadn't anticipated, and which will turn the poem in an unforeseen direction. Occasionally I can force the issue by arguing against the developing premise of the poem. Jon Anderson, one of my teachers at the University of Arizona, encouraged us to write "negative inversions," in which we would take a poem in draft and write the opposite, create a negative. If the poem began, like Auden's "September 1, 1939," with "I sit in one of the dives / On Fifty-second Street / Uncertain and afraid," you would rewrite, "I don't sit in one of the dives, etc., etc." It sounds silly performed on a great poem but it can have a dramatic and liberating result on a draft of a poem.

TGR: How about the act of organizing your work? When you're done and thinking of drawing things into a collection, how do you do that?

MC: Well, I always send the manuscript to friends for advice about the order and title, and I listen closely to what they say. When I'm assembling a manuscript I work against the obvious ways of organizing it. I'll avoid grouping poems by theme and style, wanting instead to create arcs of recognition that bind the book together. These arcs are not necessarily visible but become apparent in the course of reading the book.

In putting a manuscript together what I hope to find are moments of surprise, and also once again, resistance and tension between various poems. The overall effect is to create the impression of a single but highly variegated poem.

TGR: Let me pick up the thread you touched on, which was feedback from a group of your friends, or more broadly the role of critique. First of all, someone that has been at this as long as you have, what kind of feedback are they giving you that is useful?
MC: They give solid and honest critical responses. Some of it can be at the level of line editing, and some of it can be larger, more global issues with one or several poems. They might point out where I've failed to develop a poem enough, or have closed it off too soon, or they locate places where the diction is strained. These kinds of suggestions.

TGR: I find that quite amazing. You're open to that sort of feedback?
MC: Yes, of course. After a certain point in the process writing a poem is like building something. You've spent a lot of time working on it, and someone else can immediately see where maybe a corner isn't square. Something's not quite plumb. They point it out, and you try and put a level up against it and get it straight, bring it true. I'm happy to get criticism like that.

TGR: How many people, do you think, are in that core group of folks?
MC: It changes because it depends on who I've been talking to about the book, or who I think I can lean on at any given time. But I suppose there are probably about eight people who I would send an entire manuscript to.

TGR: I'd like to move on to your role as the director of the Bread Loaf Writers' Conference. How would you describe Bread Loaf, first of all, as an eighty-year-old institution, but also with regards to its role in letters today?
MC: I'd just been thinking about this because I've had to write a description of Bread Loaf for a Middlebury College committee

that's evaluating its summer programs. I read the director's note from the first bulletin, the first Bread Loaf Writers' Conference bulletin, 1926, describing what the conference entails. The program of lectures, seminars—what we now call workshops—and conferences was the same then as it is now. It hasn't changed very much. The emphasis has shifted away from the faculty being the central focus of the conference to the participants. But this is a shift the culture at large has made. Institutions are driven by service to their clientele and patrons.

Bread Loaf's main purpose is to encourage young and emerging writers by providing practical advice about the craft of writing, but it also has the added benefit of supporting literary writing in general. Agents, editors, and publishers visit the conference in order to educate participants about the publishing world, but their role is dwarfed by the serious way that literary writing is discussed in the lectures, workshops, and classes. The conversation about serious writing is intense and exhilarating, which has the effect of keeping everyone focused on the process—how the work gets done—more than on obtaining a publishing contract. The atmosphere of the conference is congenial and social, which helps to release some of the tension that results from the intensity of the program and the frenetic pace of the session. The spirit of the community and the sense of common purpose produced each year is very gratifying. When William Maxwell read at the conference in 1995, my first year as director, he opened his introductory remarks by saying that it seemed as if he'd found paradise. And it does seem this way, not so much because it's perfect, but because those who go feel as if they've found not only people who understand what they're doing, but who also can help them become better writers.

TGR: What does it do for you?
MC: Well, I think that at different times in your life different opportunities come along. I'm grateful for the opportunity to be associated with Bread Loaf and what it represents in the history of America's literary culture. I won't have the association forever,

but now it's what I'm devoting some of my energies to. I was hesitant to take the work on because I thought it would take away from my own work, and perhaps it has. It's hard to say. I haven't stopped writing, and I've completed a number of projects since becoming director in 1994. Bread Loaf has allowed me to familiarize myself with the next generation of American writers and to see how the writers that belong to it are developing the craft. All of this invigorates and stimulates me and has an effect on my own work.

I went to Bread Loaf in 1981 as a scholar and returned as a fellow in 1986. During those first two stays I met many writers who I've stayed in touch with. As young writers we read each other's work and challenged ourselves to change and develop artistically. It also allowed us to feel as if we were part of a larger literary landscape. Now as director of the conference, I am able to give the crucial support and encouragement that I had received from Bread Loaf to the young and emerging writers who attend. There's a great deal of satisfaction in this.

The interesting thing about Bread Loaf is that regardless of how beautiful its setting is in the Green Mountains it derives its power and magic from the people who attend. I learned this by being at the campus once in the middle of winter when no one was around, except the caretaker. I was staying in one of the houses which is kept open year round, down the hill a little bit from the main Bread Loaf campus. But, being up there, it was terrifying because it was so empty. When people are at Bread Loaf for the conference the ghosts of the place—Robert Frost, Willa Cather, Bernard DeVoto, John Gardner, Katherine Anne Porter—are palpable and present. The spirit of Bread Loaf is alive only when people are there. Otherwise, it's nothing, just a postcard-picture of a place. Actually, it's scarier than a postcard, at night at least.

TGR: Can you talk a bit about achievements, and the role of achievement for a poet?
MC: I don't want to talk about achievement [*laughs*]. Not really.

It's probably better to talk about achievements after people are dead. They're nice, they're affirmations. And yet, they make you realize, even more so, that the important thing is getting the work done, and staying connected to the work. But I don't think they're important in and of themselves. I think they can be important to people who have been ignored all their lives. Then they function as justice countering neglect. That seems to me to be the proper kind of recognition achievement should receive. But, the kind of recognition where someone has been picked out early on and gets every award that's available? Well, that creates a reputation. But it doesn't make a secure place for the work. Quite often it happens that those poets are the ones who don't last. And yet having said this, there aren't many poets, including myself, who would turn down recognition should it be given.

Another way to consider achievement is in the form of personal accomplishment. Have I accomplished everything I set out to accomplish when I started writing? Not everything, but I have written a few poems that continue to surprise and engage me. And yet, what I'm most interested in is the shape future work might take.

TGR: Can we really ever understand what work is secure, what work is going to be carried forward?

MC: No, you can't. In W. S. Merwin's poem "Berryman," a young Merwin says, "I asked how can you ever be sure / that what you write is really / any good at all and he said you can't / you can't you can never be sure / you die without knowing / whether anything you wrote was any good / if you have to be sure don't write." I subscribe to this notion, especially the high drama of Berryman's certainty. Clearly, he's thought long about this issue because he'd like to know how good he is.

It's true that we try to figure out whose work will be secure and whose won't. Poets get pushed forward and promoted by the literary establishment, let's say by Bread Loaf, and they might eventually represent the literary canon or join the curricular poets. If you look at John Hollander's great two-volume anthology of nine-teenth-century American poetry, there are only a handful of poets that you are likely to recognize. But there are many distinguished and gifted poets who produced beautiful poems, who are completely unfamiliar to us now. They got winnowed out at some point, for whatever reason, and others were promoted.

Contemporary print and digital culture allow almost anyone to publish a book. And while in the past, poets frequently paid to have work printed, the ease with which "texts" can be produced and distributed now begs the question about whether or not publishing is the credential it once was.

TGR: I'd like to dive into your work itself, which has been variously described as shocking, mysterious, and elegant, yet also clear-eyed, accessible, even colloquial. Can you talk a bit about this notion of accessibility in your work versus other approaches to poetry? For example, the mode of Language poets, perhaps?

MC: Initially, because I wanted to write fiction, and spent a lot of time trying to do that, I found myself writing poems that were based in anecdote or story or character. The issue of accessibility is a difficult one because what I take accessibility to mean is that on a certain level the poem is comprehensible to readers whose sophistication covers a wide range. Although I have to say, even with my poems, if someone doesn't read poetry much they probably won't know what's going on. But in terms of the range of poetry being written now, is mine more accessible? Probably so. What isn't necessarily as accessible is the mystery behind the poem and the necessity for writing it. I think those things are probably universal characteristics, no matter what the form, no matter what the aesthetic driving the poem. That's the common thing that holds poets together, the necessity to use language to shape experience.

TGR: We've circled back to your analogy about painting and styles of painting.

MC: Yeah, I'm happy to be simpleminded. In the end, maybe, all poets are involved in a prolonged phenomenological exercise in which all of our poems, no matter how different, are trying to get at the same thing. All approach the mystery of existence and the awe we feel at being alive. We merely use language in different ways. I trust syntax in a way that a Language or theory-based poet, to use those terms broadly, doesn't. Some of the most interesting and innovative poets writing today see syntax as a coercive agent, that its patterns force us to write in predetermined ways. In order to resist this force, which is also a social and political force, you write against syntax. One of the ways of doing this is to use fragments. I understand this as an aesthetic argument and I think I even agree with aspects of its premise. Intellectually I'm drawn to it, but emotionally I don't respond to it. I can't locate in this kind of writing the rhythm of the human voice. As a result, it is largely outside the range of my hearing.

All poetry resists language and pushes against the restrictions imposed by syntax. That's where its power comes from. All poetry resists common meaning. All poetry resists accessibility. Poetry resides in paradox, uncertainty, and contradiction, and in the contrasts and comparisons that metaphor creates.

TGR: How would you articulate William Meredith's influence on your style of, and approach to, poetry? How has he helped you illuminate poetry's role in your own life?

MC: From Meredith I learned something about decorum, about the necessity to be truthful, to avoid glibness. That language is sacred because it encapsulates the history of a people. And that poems serve the important function of refreshing and renewing language. I learned as well that there's a connection between the poet's life and work that is essential for both the integrity of the life and the work. Poetry is enriched by this connection and is useful to others in relationship to it. Meredith thought poetry was something that was useful, and that it could play a role in the advice and consent of a culture or the republic, which is why he could write a poem like "A Mild-Spoken Citizen Finally Writes to the White House." He believed in the public role of poetry. His most famous poem is "The Wreck of the Thresher." I like this idea but I don't believe in it exactly. Or I should say, I want to believe in it, but such a belief depends on an order and coherency in American culture that no longer exists. Just as it's hard to find a center in the life of the nation, it's equally difficult to find a center in American poetry.

There is no center and there's apt not ever to be a center because we are a nation more and more defined by our pluralism. This is all for the good as far as I'm concerned. It's odd that as pluralism drives the country and gives it texture, we are being ruled by a group of narrow-minded war criminals. The heart and soul of the country is as various as it's ever been, while the ruling class is more detached and removed from reality than at any other time.

TGR: A thought this triggers for me is that there isn't a center, it's fragmented, much more atomized . . .
MC: Atomized is a good way of describing it, because atoms have the ability to cohere while fragments don't. Fragments are broken, shards. I think America is atomized. And in that way, like when you atomize paint, in a spray the molecules eventually come together once they hit a surface.

TGR: So there are many centers.
MC: Yeah, I really think so. I think that's our challenge and luxury in America. To seek out a center that's meaningful and relevant to each of us.

TGR: Thank you very much for your time, Michael.
MC: It's been a pleasure.

March 2005

Acknowledgments

Earlier versions of the essays appeared in the following publications or were delivered as talks at the following venues. I am grateful to the editors who first published this work and to those who offered invitations that produced the talks.

"One Utterance: Poets on Complexity." *Crossroads: Journal of the Poetry Society of America,* Spring 2000, 24–25.

"An Exact Ratio." *Passing the Word: Writers and Their Mentors,* edited by Jeffrey Skinner. Sarabande Books, 2001.

"The Truant Pen." *Poets on Poems,* edited by Robert Pack and Jay Parini. University Press of New England, 1996.

"The Dog Gets to Dover: William Maxwell as a Correspondent." *A William Maxwell Portrait: Memoirs and Appreciations,* edited by Charles Baxter, Michael Collier, and Edward Hirsch. W. W. Norton, 2004. Also *Georgia Review,* Winter 2003.

"Becoming a Writer, Becoming a Reader." Delivered as a talk at the Hurston/Wright Awards, Richmond, Virginia, Spring 1999.

"State Flower, State Poet, State Song." *American Poet: Journal of the Academy of American Poets,* March–April 2003.

"The Look of Things." Opening Remarks, Bread Loaf Writers' Conference, 2000.

"A Final Antidote." Delivered as a lecture under the title "The Journals of Louise Bogan: The Final Antidote" at Warren Wilson College, July 1991. Also in *Virginia Quarterly Review,* Summer 2007.

"Borges and His Precursors." Delivered as a talk at the Borges Centenary Conference at the University of Maryland, February 21, 2000.

"A Strange Gratuity: On Hart Crane's 'Eternity'." *Electronic Poetry Review* 5, Winter 2003, www.poetry.org.

"On Whitman's 'To a Locomotive in Winter.'" *Virginia Quarterly Review,* Spring 2004.

"In Radical Pursuit: A Brief Appreciation" Published originally as "The Essays of Snodgrass," *Agenda* 34, no. 1: 121–22.

"Tickets for a Prayer Wheel: An Introduction." *Tickets for a Prayer Wheel,* by Annie Dillard. Wesleyan University Press, 2002.

"Widow's Choice: *Randall Jarrell's Letters.*" Edited by Mary Jarrell. *Telescope,* Winter 1985.

"The Wesleyan Tradition." Introduction to *The Wesleyan Tradition: Four Decades of American Poetry.* Wesleyan University Press, 1993.

"An Interview." *Grove Review,* On Poetry Interview Series, Fall 2005.

Grateful acknowledgment is made to the following for permission to reprint previously published materials.